The Panorama of Luke

NEIL RICHARDSON

# The Panorama of Luke

An Introduction to the Gospel of Luke
and the Acts of the Apostles

EPWORTH PRESS

7162 0374 X

First published 1982
by Epworth Press
Room 195, 1 Central Buildings, London SW1

Typeset by Gloucester Typesetting Services
and printed in Great Britain by
Richard Clay Ltd (The Chaucer Press)
Bungay, Suffolk

*To Rhiannon*

# CONTENTS

# PREFACE

The origins of this book lie in a thesis written under the supervision of Professor K. Grayston of Bristol, and I should like to express my debt to his stimulating teaching and helpful guidance. My thanks are due also to Professor Morna Hooker for her help, to my former colleague Miss Elizabeth Moore for several helpful suggestions, and to my sister Miss Jean Richardson for undertaking most of the typing.

*Manchester, October 1981*

# – I –

# Introduction:
# The Writings of Luke in Recent Scholarship

'Who wrote more of the New Testament than anyone else?' is a question to which many people would probably give the answer 'Paul'. So it is useful to remind ourselves that it was not Paul, but the man who wrote the Gospel according to Luke and the Acts of the Apostles. This is less obvious from English translations of the New Testament, since the Greek in which Paul wrote is often terse and obscure, and requires more words in translation than the more straightforward narratives of Luke and Acts. In the *New English Bible*, the writings of 'Luke' – we discuss below who he really was – occupy about 85 pages, whilst all the letters attributed to Paul fill about 87. However, few scholars today would argue that Paul wrote the letters to Timothy and Titus; one or two have suggested that the real author was the man who wrote Luke-Acts.[1] Whether he did or not, the volume of his writings would still exceed that of the epistles of Paul.

Luke, then, wrote over a quarter of the New Testament, a fact which goes some way towards justifying the large number of books which have been written about his work. In view of this, the first section of this chapter will look at some of the things which scholars have been saying.

## (i) New approaches to Luke-Acts

The traditional view of the author of Luke-Acts is still widespread and popular. According to this view, the author was Luke, the companion of Paul, who is referred to in three passages of the New Testament (Col. 4.14; II Tim. 4.11; Philem. 24), and who, according to Colossians 4.14, was a doctor. His purpose in writing what he did was to provide a reliable, historical account of the life of Jesus and of the origins of the church, and so, not surprisingly, he was thought of as a historian.

For several reasons this view has had to be modified. After the First World War, a new way of looking at the Gospels developed which recognized that the material contained in them was first passed on in bits and pieces, as it were, by word of mouth. For example, a miracle story or a parable might be adapted and used by a preacher or a teacher to meet the needs of a particular group or congregation. This may be why the parable of the Lost Sheep has come down to us in two forms (Matt. 18.12–14; Luke 15.3–7). In both versions the main body of the parable is essentially the same, but Matthew and Luke each draw different lessons from it. In Matthew the parable is a lesson for church leaders, impressing upon them the need to seek out the lapsed member (note 'these little ones' in v. 14). In Luke it is a story about God's love for the lost sinner, although Matthew does not forget that it is God's love for the lapsed member which determines the church's care for him.

It is likely that Luke's version of that parable is nearer to what Jesus himself meant by the story, but just as a preacher of any generation would draw a lesson for his congregation from a biblical passage or text, so Matthew, or the church before Matthew, adapted this parable. Many other examples could be given which suggest that before the gospels were written down, Christians used the teaching of Jesus and stories about him in the life and worship of their churches, adapting them to new situations and problems. This means that sometimes we can look at the gospels on two levels, for they may provide information not only about Jesus, but also about the early Christian communities. The story of Jesus welcoming little children (Mark 10.13–16; Matt. 19.13–15; Luke 18.15–17) may indicate that the status of children was a live issue in the first Christian communities. Why else, some scholars would argue, did Mark and the others bother to include it?

This approach to the Gospels, known as form criticism, offered another important insight. Form critics pointed out that the purpose of the 'units' which together make up a Gospel was to proclaim Jesus, rather than simply to relay information about him. That is why a single story, such as the disciples' plucking corn on the Sabbath (Mark 2.23–28; Matt. 12.1–8; Luke 6.1–5), ends with a 'punch-line': 'The Son of Man is sovereign even over the Sabbath'. Such a claim about the authority or the identity of Jesus is often the way a Gospel 'unit' ends, and in so doing it contains in a nutshell the essence of Christian faith.

This new way of looking at the Gospels can come as a jolt to those who think that the evangelists had simply written down what had happened. But whilst it is true that some scholars have been too sceptical about how much information the Gospels give us about Jesus himself, there can be no doubt that this approach is basically correct.

After form criticism there was a further development in New Testament scholarship which vitally affects our view of the Gospel writers. Scholars came to see that Mark, Matthew and Luke also adapted the stories and teaching which came to them. They were not just chroniclers, recording everything word for word, although occasionally Matthew and Luke do that;[2] they were editors who wrote things down in their own way, modifying here and there, or even rewriting, in order to make a particular point, or because they wanted their readers to see things in a certain light. As this approach was concerned mainly with how and why the Gospels were edited, i.e. redacted, it became known as redaction criticism. So the Gospel writers began to be thought of not so much as historians, but as theologians. That is to say, their writings do not simply convey information about Jesus; they are proclamations, reflecting the writers' own convictions about him.

In the light of all this, it is not surprising that the traditional view of Luke-Acts as a fairly straightforward historical account began to be questioned. But there are other reasons, too, for questioning that view. Although it is convenient to refer to the author of Luke-Acts as 'Luke', we cannot be certain that it was Luke, the companion of Paul, who wrote it. He may have done, but the title alone does not prove that he did, since it was the custom then to put the name of a well-known person at the top of the papyrus roll of which a book would consist. It is perfectly possible that the author used some material which had been written by the real Luke, or wrote up what Luke told him, but there are differences between the Acts of the Apostles and the epistles of Paul which at least raise doubts about whether Acts – and therefore Luke-Acts, since few believe that the two volumes were written by different authors – could have been written by someone who knew Paul. And so here we must anticipate the arguments of a later section of this book (Chapter 5, i) by looking at a few of these discrepancies.

In the first two chapters of his letter to the Galatians, Paul lists the number of times he had been to Jerusalem since he became a Christian. But what he says does not tally with the number of such journeys mentioned in Acts, which has one extra.[3] Had Paul forgotten about this visit, or did Luke get his facts wrong? The latter seems more likely, especially as there are other details in Acts which suggest that the writer did not know Paul, or at least did not fully understand his views. For example, would Paul have called himself a Pharisee (compare Acts 23.6 and Phil. 3.5–7), or expressed his conviction about justification by faith in the way that he is made to do in Acts 13.38f.? Scholars are divided about these and other similar matters, but the evidence seems, on balance, to favour those who think that Acts was written by someone who did not know Paul personally.

Some will wish to argue that the presence of the word 'we' in Acts proves that it was written by someone who was with Paul. For example, Acts 16.10 reads, 'After he had seen this vision, we at once set about getting a passage to Macedonia, concluding that God had called us to bring them the good news.' At first sight this, and many other verses in the second half of Acts, seems to show that the author was personally involved in what he is describing. However, there are one or two curious facts to be taken into consideration. First, the word 'we' appears and disappears rather mysteriously; altogether it is to be found in Acts 16.10–17; 20.5–15; 21.1–18; and finally in most of the last two chapters (27.1–28.16). Could these passages be Luke's way of indicating unobtrusively events at which he himself was present? Some think so, but there is another explanation. Scholars have noticed for a long time that the 'we' appears when Paul embarks on a major voyage at sea, and fades out fairly soon after he disembarks. It is possible that the author of Acts was using a diary or log-book at these points, and retained the 'we' in order to acknowledge that he had done so, but recent research suggests otherwise. Ever since Homer wrote *The Odyssey* it had been the custom for Greek authors to describe sea-voyages in the first person plural. It became a literary tradition partly, no doubt, because the first person style was more vivid, recapturing more effectively the adventure of such voyages. (And in the ancient world, all sea-voyages of any length were much more challenging and forbidding than they are today.) This is the likeliest explanation of 'we' in Acts; the author adopted what was then the traditional style for voyages at sea.[4]

For many reasons, therefore, opinions about the writings of Luke have changed a good deal in the last fifty years, and in the last three decades scholars have concentrated on the study of Luke as a theologian, rather than Luke the historian. But it is not a case of 'either-or'. The differences between Acts and Paul do not mean that Luke was a careless, wildly inaccurate historian who cannot be trusted. The real calibre of his work will emerge as we proceed. Suffice it to say here that in our approach to Luke we would be wise to lay aside modern notions of history-writing and not to be surprised if Luke does not seem to have been as critical or as accurate as we think he should have been. There are places where he plainly got his facts wrong – for example, his references to Theudas and Judas (Acts 5.36f.)[5] – and others, e.g. Luke 5.12, where the precise geographical details do not seem to have been his concern.

At the same time Luke shows an undoubted flair for background 'colour', and it has been pointed out how accurate are his local government references in Acts. He knew that Philippi had the status of a Roman colony (Acts 16.12) and that the local magistrates at Thessalonica were called 'politarchs' (Acts 17.8). But we shall be wasting our time if we expend too much effort in either querying or defending the accuracy of Luke. The value of his writings for Christian faith does not depend on his getting a 'first' in history.

We have looked at some of the reasons why opinions about Luke have changed. It is now time to consider briefly some of the books which scholars have written about him in the last thirty years. The man whose work has perhaps had the greatest influence is a German scholar, Hans Conzelmann. A book first published in 1953, translated into English in 1960 and published as *The Theology of Saint Luke*, argues that Luke was greatly influenced by the delay in the return of Jesus and in the final coming of the kingdom. He and his Christian contemporaries, Conzelmann believes, did not think that the world would come to a speedy end as Paul, for one, had thought (see, for example, I Thess. 4.13–17), and so Luke offered his reader a way of understanding the continuing history of salvation. First, there was the time of preparation for Christ, the period of the law and the prophets (Luke 16.16). Then came the time of salvation (Luke 4.18–21), the time of Jesus' own ministry. From Luke's standpoint this had become the centre of history, a kind of 'middle time', for it had now been succeeded by the time of the church, stretching indefinitely into the future and marked by very different conditions from those which obtained during Jesus' lifetime (Luke 22.35–38).

This is the dominant idea of Conzelmann's book, although there are discussions in it of many other aspects of Luke's thought. Some, such as his view that many of the geographical details in the Gospel are imbued with a symbolic, or theological meaning, are questionable, but it is Conzelmann more than any other scholar who has promoted the view that Luke was first and foremost a theologian.

In some ways this approach is an advance on the old. It recognizes that Luke did not copy down everything word for word, but reshaped the material available to him. In particular it is possible to see how he altered Mark, if we anticipate for a moment the view, discussed below, that Mark's Gospel was one of his sources.

In the earliest Gospel Jesus begins his ministry by saying, 'The time has come' (1.15), whereas in Luke Jesus' opening message is, 'The Spirit of the Lord is upon me' (Luke 4.18), and a message similar to that of Jesus in Mark is attributed to false prophets (21.8). Conzelmann rightly argues that changes such as this mark a fundamental change of perspective.

All this may seem very disturbing, but it need not be so. We cannot by-pass completely the questions 'What actually happened?' and 'What did Jesus himself say?', although firm answers are not always possible, but the view of Luke as a theologian encourages us to read his work on a level deeper than that of mere historical narrative. He has, it is true, presented his work as history in some respects (1.1-4 and 3.1), but if he is more than a mere chronicler we have to ask of his work not simply 'What does he say happened?', but primarily, 'What convictions about Christ or the Christian life is he expressing?'

Such a view of Luke has become almost orthodox, particularly amongst German scholars, but there have been criticisms of Conzelmann's work. It can be shown that Luke's writings do not reflect a fully-worked-out systematic theology, and it may be that his theological achievement has been exaggerated. It is important that we should derive insights and guidance from Luke in working out our own theology today, but what we find in his writings may not have been in his mind at all, even though we may be perfectly justified in reading what we do out of his work. Secondly, there is such a rich variety of material in the narratives of Luke-Acts that we cannot be sure that he has employed it all in the service of his theology. We noted earlier that Luke occasionally, at least, copied his sources fairly closely, and he may well have included some stories or teaching in his work simply because they were part of the tradition he knew.

The book by Conzelmann is the most important and influential example of German scholarship, along with a very large commentary on Acts by Ernst Haenchen,[6] whose views are similar to Conzelmann's, although he recognizes that Luke's theology is relatively simple and unsophisticated. There are several books by British scholars, however, which diverge rather more from Conzelmann. Howard Marshall argues that Luke was both a theologian and a historian, and certainly it would be foolish to argue that he has to be one or the other. Eric Franklin, in his book *Christ the Lord*, points out, against Conzelmann, that there are places in Luke's writings where Christ's return seems to be expected in the near future (e.g. Luke 12.40), and that the delay in his return, so far from extending into the future, is now over. This does more justice to the varied material in Luke-Acts, since account has to be taken of apparent inconsistencies in Luke's work.

In Franklin's book there are several valuable correctives to widespread but mistaken views about Luke-Acts. It has been commonly thought, for example, that Luke wished to present Christianity in as favourable a light as possible to Rome, and to portray the Roman authorities equally favourably too. Some texts support this, but others (e.g. Luke 22.35ff. and Acts 24.26f.) do not. Similarly, Franklin is surely right in pointing to the variety in Luke's teaching about wealth and poverty; this teaching cannot be reduced to one simple rule. Lastly, he recognizes Luke's great debt to the Old Testament, and the limitations of language which that imposes on him.

Another writer who stresses the influence of the Old Testament upon Luke is John Drury, whose views, expressed in his book *Tradition and Design in Luke's Gospel*, agree at many points with those of the present writer. (I would dissent, however, from his view that Luke knew and borrowed from the Gospel of Matthew.) In his second chapter, 'A Place on the Map', Drury groups Luke's work with the later writings of the New Testament such as the Letter to the Hebrews and the Letters to Timothy and Titus. The Pastoral Epistles, especially, reflect a situation where the church has, to some extent, come to terms with the world, notably in the way in which Christians are encouraged to pray for kings and rulers (I Tim. 2.1f.). Luke's view of the Jewish Law is also as uncomplicated as that expressed in the Pastorals (e.g. I Tim. 1.9), unlike the tortuous arguments developed by Paul in his letters to the Romans and to the Galatians.

One further book may be mentioned here. Some time ago theories were put forward suggesting that Matthew and John wrote their Gospels to be read in their churches section by section as part of a lectionary cycle. Now Michael Goulder has put forward a similar argument for Luke. In his book *The Evangelists' Calendar*, he suggests that Luke wrote his Gospel having in mind the Old Testament lectionary cycles used by both church and synagogue. Goulder argues his case in great detail, believing that there are correspondences in themes between Luke and the various Old Testament readings. It must be said, however, that these often seem slight, and Goulder's interpretation of Luke's preface, fairly crucial to his case, is open to question.[7]

Nevertheless, scholars such as Goulder have contributed much to our understanding and knowledge of the writer of Luke-Acts and his background. Their approach, however much their views might be open to modification and criticism, represents an advance on the old traditional view to which we cannot, in all honesty, now return. We may, of course, conclude eventually that 'Luke the Theologian' is as incomplete a title for Luke as 'Luke the Historian'; much depends on what we mean by 'theologian'. We indicated earlier one or two defects in this approach, which might easily overlook not only the apparent contradictions in Luke's thought, but also difficult verses and stories which are often neglected. For this reason we shall survey some of the stranger features of Luke-Acts, asking what Luke understood by them, and what are the implications of their presence in the New Testament.

But first it is necessary to try to present a 'thumb-nail' sketch of Luke's purpose, situation and methods.

## (ii) 'My dear Theophilus . . .'

When we ask what Luke was trying to do, it would clearly be sensible to look first at what he himself says in his preface (Luke 1.1–4), which was probably the preface to both Luke and Acts (unless the second volume was an afterthought). It is addressed to 'Theophilus', who may have been an individual known to Luke, but we have no means of determining who he was. The name, however, meant 'Friend of God', and so it is possible that this was Luke's way of dedicating his book to the church or, more probably, to his own local church. Whether this was so or not, the local church was no doubt the 'audience' Luke had in mind first and foremost, although he may have hoped to win a wider readership. And so if we imagine Luke as a member of a large, thriving church in one of the great cities of the central or eastern Mediterranean, we should not be far wrong. Corinth and Ephesus were two such cities, but as the narrative of Acts ends in the imperial capital, Rome, it is as likely a candidate as any.

The preface proceeds as follows: 'Many writers have undertaken to draw up an account of the events that have happened among us.' This suggests that Luke thought he could do better than his predecessors. He would hardly have undertaken such a task if he and his church possessed what they thought were perfectly satisfactory accounts of the life of the early church. Unfortunately only two, at the most, of these earlier writers survive, namely the Gospels of Mark and Matthew. Whether Luke knew Matthew or not – and that is debatable – it is not likely that he would have regarded it as suitable for his own situation. Matthew probably wrote for Jewish Christians, whereas Luke, for all his Old Testament background, was writing either for Gentiles, or for Jews and Gentiles, and he may have felt that some verses in Matthew were difficult, to say the least. What would his readers have made of Matt. 7.6 ('Do not give dogs what is holy' – 'dog' being the Jewish term of opprobrium for a Gentile), or of Matt. 10.5 ('Do not take the road to Gentile lands' – the command of Jesus to the disciples)?

The other Gospel written before Luke was that of Mark. Later on we shall note more of the alterations which Luke made to the text of Mark, but it is clear from these, from the omissions (notably Mark 6.45–8.26), and from the addition of, for example, much more teaching, that Luke wanted to replace Mark with a Gospel which was better written and more comprehensive.

The preface continues: '. . . following the traditions handed down to us by the original eye-witnesses and servants of the gospel.' Comparisons with other prefaces written by other Greek and Roman historians have shown that this is a conventional preface. To some extent Luke is saying the usual things, and so it is difficult to know how much weight to place on individual words. However, there may be a clue here to the time when Luke was writing. He has been described as a 'third generation' Christian, like the writer to the Hebrews, who implied that there was a generation of apostles and eyewitnesses between the time of Jesus and his own time (2.3f.). In other words, not only is the time of Jesus' earthly ministry over, but so too is the age of the apostles. This may have been partly why Luke took up his pen. Time was passing, and Christian origins were receding further and further into the past. They seemed far away not only in time, but also in distance, since Judaea must have seemed a small, far-away country to some of Luke's contemporaries in Corinth or Rome, if that was where he wrote.

'And so I in my turn, your Excellency, as one who has gone over the whole course of these events in detail . . .' The most interesting Greek word here is the one rather colourlessly translated by the phrase 'one who has gone over'. A more literal translation would be 'one who has followed everything from the start', but what does that mean? That Luke followed closely what other people had said or written, or that he was actually involved in what he was describing? The word is ambiguous, but in the light of our earlier arguments, the first meaning is more likely.

'. . . have decided to write a connected narrative for you, so as to give you authentic knowledge about the matters of which you have been informed.' Again there are several ambiguous words here. The word translated by 'have been informed' is one such, since it may mean no more than the *New English Bible* translation implies, but it could also mean that Theophilus was a catechumen – i.e. one being trained in Christian faith for baptism and full membership of the church. Finally, we should note the phrase 'authentic knowledge'. In the Greek this comes last in the sentence, which means that Luke wished to emphasize it. Perhaps we might paraphrase the last part, 'so that you may have the truth and nothing but the truth about the Christian faith'.

In short, there is much to be said for the view that Luke was writing towards the end of the first century in Rome or another great city of the Roman Empire. He wrote, not as a companion of Paul, but as one for whom Paul was a true hero of the faith, however imperfectly he understood the complexities of Paul's theology. And he wrote, not simply as a historian, but in order to supply his contemporaries with a Gospel which they could regard as theirs, and in order to bridge the growing gap between the time of Jesus and their own.

These conclusions inevitably cannot be certain or final, and though they would command the general assent of many scholars, not all will agree with them. There is even more disagreement about Luke's methods and sources, and it will be necessary to outline briefly the main questions which are debated in this area as well.

The problems chiefly concern the Gospel, since the sources Luke used for his second volume, in spite of much research, have not been discerned or discovered. Most scholars, although not all, are agreed that Luke used Mark; there seems to be some literary connection between the two Gospels, and the differences are most easily explained by the theory that Luke borrowed from Mark. For example, it is not too difficult to understand why Luke omitted the phrases and sections of Mark which are not found in his Gospel;[8] it is much harder to appreciate why Mark would omit such a large amount of Luke's material, and produce a Gospel less than two-thirds the size of Luke's.

But what were the other sources of the third evangelist? Some argue that Luke also borrowed from Matthew's Gospel; if he did, that means he did a considerable amount of re-writing and re-arranging, including a drastic dissection of the Sermon on the Mount.[9] It also means that, as Matthew's Gospel has a fairly clear pattern to it, with blocks of teaching and healings, Luke must have re-arranged it with another pattern in mind. The heart of the problem lies in the so-called central section of his Gospel (9.51–18.14), which contains very little, if anything, from Mark. Some, including John Drury and Michael Goulder, think that Luke modelled this section on the book of Deuteronomy in the Old Testament, but it is not self-evident, and the case remains far from proven. The apparent lack of any clear structure in this part of the Gospel remains the greatest obstacle to the view that Luke borrowed from Matthew.

Another, longer-standing debate concerns the order in which Luke used his sources. Did he write a first edition of his Gospel, and then, after discovering Mark's Gospel, a second larger edition which included most of his new 'find'? This may seem to be a singularly unimportant and irrelevant debate, and so it would be if very little time elapsed between Luke's first and second editions. But if Luke's first draft of his Gospel was written ten or fifteen years earlier than the final version, it might be, in effect, our earliest Gospel, and so the oldest record of the life and teaching of Jesus. The evidence is extremely complicated,[10] but if we reject the view that the author of Luke's Gospel was the travelling-companion of Paul, this 'Proto-Luke' theory, as it is called, becomes virtually untenable.

One final point must be added here. Luke brought to his work a first-rate talent for writing. He tells stories with consummate artistry; one memorable picture after another is presented to his readers vividly, colourfully, and often dramatically. It is hardly surprising that Christians of later centuries came to believe that he had been an artist. He varies his style to suit his subject. At one point it owes everything to the Old Testament – the first two chapters of his Gospel are the supreme example of this. At another his style reflects the atmosphere of Greece's venerable seat of learning, Athens (Acts 17.16–34).

Luke's skill in writing goes a long way towards explaining the enormous influence he has had on the church. The development of the Christian year, especially the sequence Easter, Ascension, Pentecost, we owe to him, since he is the only New Testament writer who distinguishes three events of this kind. But perhaps he has exercised his most profound influence, in modern times no less than in previous generations, by the way in which his writings have enabled people to picture in their mind's eye the life of Jesus and the origins of the Christian church.

It did not take the church long to decide that Luke's writings had a pre-eminent authority. There were many writings jostling for a place in that select group of documents we now call the New Testament, and several centuries passed before the church finally decided which should be included and which should be excluded. Revelation and the Letter to the Hebrews were two documents which only just scraped into the canon. But from at least the end of the second century there was never any doubt that Luke-Acts belonged in the 'first division' of Christian writings. There were many other Gospels (the Gospel of Peter, the Gospel of Thomas, etc.), and many other 'Acts' (the Acts of Peter, the Acts of Paul, etc.), but eventually most Christians concluded that four Gospels towered over the rest, and that only one Acts, the Acts of the Apostles, deserved to be included in the exalted company of Gospels and Epistles. This fact alone suggests that it is well worth while asking what the meaning of Luke's writings might be for us today.

# – 2 –

# From Nazareth to Jerusalem

At the beginning of our study of Luke's first volume we need to consider a little more the implications of the approach to the Gospels known as redaction criticism. This approach has enabled us to see the writers of the Gospels as men who brought to their work their own ideas and convictions about Jesus, each writing his Gospel in the way that he thought best. If that is so, we need not be surprised at the differences between them.

These differences have often been explained by using the illustration of newspaper reports. Three journalists would report the same incident in varying ways, and so why shouldn't the Gospel writers? But this analogy is misleading for two reasons. First, the aims of the evangelists were different from those of a modern newspaper reporter. Admittedly, a journalist may 'slant' his news in a particular way, but the Gospel writers were doing much more than that. Secondly, these three writers, unlike journalists, were not working independently of each other. Matthew and Luke almost certainly drew upon Mark's Gospel, and, if Luke did not use Matthew, he and Matthew must have had another source, or sources, which they both used as well. So we have to reckon with the at first disconcerting fact that Luke and Matthew deliberately altered Mark when and where they saw fit to do so, and, we may presume, did the same with whatever other sources were available. Was this because they felt that they had more reliable information? If we compare them carefully, it seems that this may sometimes have been the reason behind their alterations, but not usually. For example, Matthew and Luke each narrate the healing of the centurion's servant (Matt. 8.5–13; Luke 7.1–10). Matthew says that the centurion approached Jesus directly, Luke that he communicated with him via Jewish intermediaries. If they both used the same source, is it possible to see why one of them might have altered it? In fact, it seems likely that Luke did so, since never once in his Gospel does Jesus come into contact with a Gentile (see section i below).

This is only one amongst many possible examples. We might compare also Mark 1.35–38 and Luke 4.42f., in which, according to Mark, the earlier Gospel, it is Peter and the disciples who 'hound' Jesus, as the Greek implies. But in Luke's version the crowds simply look for him. And yet Luke had Mark's Gospel in front of him.

In short, the evangelists often altered their sources because they wished to make a particular theological point, or in order to present Christian truth from a fresh angle. And so, rather than think of them as historians or reporters, we should regard them as editors, perhaps even as theologians, but certainly as artists, each engaged on his own portrait of Jesus. We shall need to explore later both the challenge and the value of this approach, but to begin with, we shall attempt to outline some of the distinctive features of Luke's Gospel.

## (i) Past and future

After his carefully worded preface, Luke abruptly changed style. It is as if a modern writer had switched from the style on the dust-jacket of his book to that of the Authorized Version. And so with one phrase, 'And it came to pass, in the days of Herod the king', Luke whisked his readers away from the cultured Greek world of his introduction to that of the Old Testament.

A survey of the first two chapters of the Gospel shows that there are echoes of the Old Testament and allusions to it everywhere. Zacharias and Elizabeth are described in terms reminiscent of Abram and Sarai, details such as the foetus moving in Elizabeth's womb (1.41 and 44) are taken from the Old Testament (Gen. 25.22); the Magnificat (1.46–55) is modelled on the Song of Hannah (I Sam. 2.1–10); the boy Jesus is described in language echoing words used of Samuel (2.52; I Sam. 2.26), and so on. The influence of the Jewish scriptures on Luke's style, language and ideas can hardly be exaggerated.

What is Luke trying to do here? It is important, first, that we appreciate what kind of writing this is. Luke was probably writing a piece of 'haggadah', that is, a devout meditation based upon the scriptures. However much there may be a historical nucleus to these chapters – e.g. John's parents may well have been called Zacharias and Elizabeth – the end-product and the overall impression is largely due to Luke's Christian imagination. In fact, what he has given us is a series of tableaux which present in a way both beautiful and profound the significance of the birth of Christ. The word 'significance' is important, for Luke's concern was the meaning and relevance of it all, which mattered far more than whether there really were shepherds present at the nativity.

What, then, can be learned from these tableaux? First, what is Luke saying to his readers through the story of Zacharias and Elizabeth? It is something like this: just as the first stage of Israel's pilgrimage in the world began when God gave a son to an ageing, childless couple, so now he repeats himself. By adopting an Old Testament style, Luke implies that God is consistent, and will not abandon what he has begun in the past. But this time the new-born child will mark the inauguration of the last, decisive stage of Israel's history. To show that this is a new beginning, he will receive the Holy Spirit (1.15), for not since the time of the last prophets had the Spirit been given to Israel. And so for the first, but by no means the last, time in Luke-Acts, continuity with the past is asserted. Indeed, Luke makes it increasingly clear that in his view the Old Testament and Christian faith are quite inseparable.

When we turn to the account of the birth of Jesus and the preparation for it, we come to the best-known section of Luke's Jewish 'haggadah'. All the traditional, popular representations of the Nativity derive largely, if not entirely, from Luke 2.1–20. Yet the sentiment which these verses attract each year could hardly be further from their real thrust. I have suggested that they may be largely the product of Luke's imagination, but the real point is not whether they are fact or fiction. It is what they mean. And here Luke intended to anticipate the way of a Messiah who ministered to outcasts (in this case shepherds), whose life from start to finish was one of poverty and humility, and who by these means initiated a revolution in human affairs. The 'cutting-edge' of the Gospel, therefore, which emerges so clearly later on (see Chapter 3, i), is not absent here either, and is sharply expressed in the hymn of Mary: 'The hungry he has satisfied with good things, the rich sent empty away' (1.53).

The number of Old Testament echoes diminishes after the first two chapters, but there are still plenty of them. In the raising of the son of a widow at Nain, Luke employs a phrase used of Elijah and Elisha (7.15; I Kings 17.23; II Kings 4.36), and Jesus' departure for Jerusalem (9.51) is described in Old Testament phrases. Such a deeply scriptural style continues until halfway through Acts, when Luke begins to narrate the moving out of the gospel into the larger Mediterranean world, and from then onwards he writes in a Greek which is more secular.

Luke's Jewishness[1] can be seen not only in the style of his writing. He shared many contemporary Jewish beliefs about angels, such as the conviction that they guarded the righteous (Luke 22.43f.; Acts 12.7ff.); that a man has a personal guardian angel (Acts 12.15); that angels carried out God's punishment of the wicked (Acts 12.23) and relayed messages from God to man (e.g. Luke 1.26) and prayers from man to God. (Luke may not have held this last-mentioned belief, but Acts 10.4 is remarkably like two verses in the Apocrypha, Tobit 12.12 and 15.)

More important for our understanding of his work, Luke appears to have regarded Jerusalem as the holy city. This was almost certainly reverence in retrospect, since the Romans had destroyed it in AD 70, but Luke's veneration for the religious capital of Judaism explains why it is the centre of things for him far more than for Matthew or Mark. The opening and closing scenes of Luke 1 and 2 take place in Jerusalem, and the 'liberation' of the city (2.38) is the fervent hope of all devout Jews. The third and final temptation takes place there (contrast Matt. 4.1–13 and Luke 4.1–13), the resurrection appearances occur there, and in Acts Jerusalem is represented as the Christian 'HQ', with all the authority that implies.

One other instance of Luke's Jewishness may be noted here. In Matthew and Mark Jesus occasionally, though not often, meets Gentiles. In both these Gospels, for example, he heals the daughter of a Syro-Phoenician woman (Mark 7.24–30; Matt. 15.21–28). Luke has omitted this story. In the story of the healing of the centurion's servant, as we saw, Luke probably rewrote the introduction in order to keep Jesus away from Gentiles entirely. It is difficult to be sure what Jesus himself actually did in this matter, but Luke, over-tidily perhaps, regarded the period up to the resurrection as the time of the Jews. Only then does the time of the Gentiles begin.

Luke himself may have been a Gentile; it is impossible to be sure. But the Jewishness of his writings is very striking. He shows not the slightest wish to disown the Jewish ancestry of his faith, but only a profound appreciation of it. A superficial reading of the opening chapters of the Gospel might suggest that Luke was motivated by no more than a romantic nostalgia towards the Old Testament. But it is more likely that he deeply believed that the Christian faith could not disown or sit lightly to its past without becoming a quite different religion.

If that is how Luke viewed the past, what were his thoughts about the future? Here we find a significant difference from Mark, who wrote before the Romans destroyed Jerusalem in AD 70, and who may have expected the end of the world at the same time as that impending catastrophe. Indeed, he may have written in the belief that the world had but a year or two to run its course.

Luke was a Christian of the next generation, and saw things quite differently, as Conzelmann, the German scholar, argued (Chapter 1, i). The opening pronouncement of Jesus is not 'The time is fulfilled', as it is in Mark, and although Luke still urged his readers to watch and pray (e.g. Luke 12.35), he seemed to have in mind a longer interval before the end of the world. That may be implied in the opening verses of Acts, where the disciples are directed, not to wait for the restoration of Israel, or to gaze into the heavens in expectation of Christ's return, but to preach the Gospel to the ends of the earth (Acts 1.1–11).

Luke's different outlook involved him in rewriting Mark's Gospel at certain points. He could hardly do otherwise when he came to Mark 13, since Jerusalem had fallen, but the world still went on its way (see, for example, the differences between Mark 13.14–24 and Luke 21.20–25).[2] For the same reason the Christian life is portrayed rather differently in Luke's writings. It becomes much more a 'pilgrim's progress': '. . . to enter the kingdom of God we must pass through many hardships' (Acts 14.22). The Christian faith itself is described as 'the Way' (e.g. Acts 9.2), in which endurance is vital. The community of the last days becomes in Luke a people on pilgrimage.

So Luke has given us a Gospel, and more than a Gospel, on a grand scale. The style of his opening chapters and the genealogy (3.23–38) show that he regarded the coming of Jesus as both a fulfilment and a continuation of what God had been doing since the time of Abraham, and even since creation began. In this way Jesus becomes for him the centre of history. All time before him was a period of preparation; all time since his coming is the era of fulfilment. Our modern understanding of evolution, so far from undermining Luke's panorama, only serves to make it more impressive.

(ii) The divine plan

This sub-title is used also by G. B. Caird in the introduction to his commentary;[3] in many ways it is an apt title for the whole of Luke's work. This, too, is part of Luke's perspective, and the two volumes as a whole convey a powerful impression of the onward march of events, directed from start to finish by God.

Leaving aside the birth of John the Baptist, which was the indispensable preparation for what followed, we come to the story of the miraculous conception of Jesus, the so-called virgin birth. It is well-known that these verses in Luke (1.34f.), and a passage in Matthew (1.18–25), are the only references in the New Testament to this subject. It is also clear that Christians can and do differ widely in what they believe about this. What, however, can be said in the light of Luke's writing, is that by this story he asserted that the contribution of God, as it were, to the birth of Jesus was more important that the role of Joseph. But just as the Hebrew way of saying that the disciple must love Christ more than his family was to say, 'If anyone comes to me and does not hate his father and mother . . .' (Luke 14.26), so here Luke is saying, 'God, not Joseph', instead of 'God more than Joseph'.

The cosmic significance of the birth of Jesus is made plain by various touches. The census, although Luke may have got his facts wrong here,[4] is important in putting the event in the context of the Roman Empire (2.1); the song of the angels declares that the earth is the recipient of God's favour (2.14); and Simeon's song anticipates the world-wide influence which this birth will have (2.32).

The impression that it is God who is behind it all continues to be given in the account of Jesus' baptism. Luke's originality here lies in leaving out John the Baptist altogether! What happened on this occasion, he seems to be saying, was something between God and Jesus alone. The role of the Baptist was unimportant compared with a sign from God himself that a new phase of his work was about to begin. Yet before Luke starts his account of Jesus' ministry, he cannot resist indicating once more the majestic sweep of the divine plan by the genealogy of Jesus (3.23–38). Whether he knew of Matthew's genealogy or not, he was obviously not content to stop at Abraham in tracing Jesus' ancestry, but went further back still to the first man, Adam, and finally to God himself.

So far there have been only hints of conflict and opposition in the words of Simeon to Mary and in the fate of John the Baptist (2.34f.; 3.19f.). Luke never lets his readers doubt for one moment that God will see his plan through to a triumphant conclusion. But with chapter 4 the conflict has begun in earnest. The dramatic encounter of Jesus with Satan (4.1–13) brings into sharp relief the nature of Jesus' ministry, and the way in which he will execute God's plan. Three short-cuts are dangled temptingly before him: give the people just what they want, compromise your way to power, or play the superman. The temptations are rejected, but the reader is warned that we have not seen the last of Satan.

The alternative, almost the blueprint of the divine plan, is presented in the following verses (4.18–30). There can be little doubt that Luke wanted his readers to see here, in words taken with minor alterations from the book of Isaiah, the manifesto for Jesus' entire ministry:

> The Spirit of the Lord is upon me because he has anointed me;
> He has sent me to announce good news to the poor,
> To proclaim release for prisoners and recovery of sight for the blind;
> To let the broken victims go free,
> To proclaim the year of the Lord's favour (4.18f.).

Jesus is the Spirit-filled man *par excellence*; that is the secret of a creative power which brings to people both freedom and wholeness. Where these things happen in human life, there the work of Christ is done, and the divine plan fulfilled.

The vast majority of the stories in both the Gospel and Acts are simply the implementation of this manifesto, but the miracle stories found only in Luke's Gospel especially highlight these themes. Jesus restores to life the dead son of a widow at Nain (7.11–17); a woman who had been a prostitute finds forgiveness because she loved much (7.39–50); a woman called Mary, who had been at the mercy of inner forces she could not control ('possessed' was the contemporary term), was healed (8.2); another woman who had a crippling weakness of the spine was restored to health, against all the religious scruples of the day, on the sabbath (13.10–17); ten social outcasts – such was the fate of a leper – were also healed (17.11–19). These comprise most of the healing stories which are found in Luke but in no other Gospel. It is significant that in all of them except one it is a woman who is healed, and in the exception a Samaritan is singled out for special mention (17.16). Along with Gentiles and slaves, women were regarded by the average Jew (and not only Jews) as second-class human beings, whilst Samaritans were the victims of that particular odium which seems to be reserved for those regarded as racial and religious half-castes. Yet all these, according to Luke, were the recipients of what Jesus had to give.

Healing – both physical and spiritual – continues to the very end in this Gospel. At the last stop before Jerusalem, one who had been an avaricious quisling is persuaded to part with his ill-gotten gains in response to Jesus (19.1–10). Even in Gethsemane one of 'the enemy' is healed (22.50f.), and from the cross a thief receives a benediction (23.43). Finally, there is a hint, though no more than a hint, that the death of Jesus, too, is part of his healing work. What is the 'exodus' mentioned in the transfiguration (9.31)? Is Luke referring to Jesus' own 'exit' from the world, or to another exodus when a nation of slaves was led to freedom?

In the healing ministry of Jesus Luke invited his readers to see God at work. If we wish to understand the divine plan in history, this is one of the most important places to look. But it was too much for some. Jesus' healing activity cut across conventional barriers, flouted contemporary religious rules, extended to the most unlikely characters. This will always be too much for those who cannot see that the work of God consists in precisely this: the healing of broken lives (see, for example, 5.17–26).

But for others it did not seem to be enough. Two disciples are portrayed as saying wistfully, '. . . we had been hoping that he was the man to liberate Israel' (24.21), and John the Baptist himself inquired, doubtfully perhaps, 'Are you the one . . .?' (7.19). After all, a divine intervention would make more of a mark on the world stage than this! It would surely be easier to believe in a God who threw his weight around, imposed his stamp firmly on things, put sinners decisively in their place . . . But to those who think thus the challenging reply is given: 'Go . . . and tell John what you have seen and heard: how the blind recover their sight, the lame walk . . . and happy is the man who does not find me a stumbling-block' (7.22). Jesus might not represent the kind of God they wanted, but the question is posed whether here might not be the kind of God they needed.

(iii) Learners and witnesses

Luke, writing almost certainly later than Mark and Matthew, began his Gospel when few, if any, of the apostles were still alive, and Christian origins may have seemed to be receding out of memory. This is one reason why he portrayed the disciples rather differently from the other Gospel writers. For him they were the founding fathers of the church, the vital link between the time of Jesus and his own day. So they are not the rather obtuse, self-centred individuals described by Mark, but God's chosen witnesses who would continue the mission of Jesus after the resurrection.

First, the call of the disciples (5.1–11), of whom Peter is, as always, the leader and spokesman, is not simply a call; it is a conversion. The words of Peter, 'Go, Lord, leave me, sinner that I am!', denote the repentance without which, in Luke's view, discipleship could not really begin. This was Peter's response to the miraculous catch of fish, which inevitably raises problems for many modern readers. Was it a legend, or had it a basis in fact? Mark has a quite different account of the call of the disciples (1.16–20), and Luke's version is strangely like the resurrection appearance described in John's Gospel (21.1–14). So our questions cannot be answered with any certainty, nor can we be sure whether, if something like this did happen, it took place before or after the resurrection. As usual, it is the message which matters, and here the miraculous catch of fish anticipates the future work of the disciples, which would be equally impossible without divine assistance.

The formal choosing of the Twelve (6.12–16) reflects Luke's understanding of their high vocation. Jesus spent the night in prayer beforehand. It was because Luke saw the apostles as the men of the future that he eliminated some of the faults which Mark attributed to them. The searing words of Jesus to Peter, 'Away with you, Satan' (Mark 8.33; Matt. 16.23), find no place in this Gospel, and at the end, it seems, Luke cannot bring himself to say that the disciples ran away (compare Mark 14.48–53 with Luke 22.52–54).

Yet it can easily be forgotten that even in Luke the disciples are far from paragons of virtue. James and John were guilty of the greatest 'gaffe' in wanting Jesus to emulate Elijah's blood-and-thunder tactics (Luke 9.54; II Kings 1.10); all the disciples argue to the last about who is the greatest (9.46; 22.24), and show intolerance to someone not of their number doing the work of Christ (9.49); lastly, the threefold denial of Jesus by Peter is recounted (22.54–71).

These are the people who accompanied Jesus from Galilee to Jerusalem. For Luke that journey was a very significant one, because Galilee was the place where it all began (Luke 23.5; Acts 10.37), and so it mattered that there should be men who had witnessed everything. Their record, as we have seen, was anything but unblemished, and yet the most significant word of all had still to be spoken:

You are the men who have stood firmly by me in my times of trial; and now I vest in you the kingship which my Father vested in me; you shall eat and drink at my table in my kingdom and sit on thrones as judges of the twelve tribes of Israel (22.28–30).

These words agree with Luke's understanding of the unique position of
the apostles in the church. They had not earned it or qualified for it,
and yet it was theirs. Those verses, in fact, suggest that power and
authority were the chief legacies of Jesus to his apostles, and so we must
go on to ask, if that is so, whether Luke saw them as an ecclesiastical
élite distinguished by the power they wielded.

Several features of the Gospel suggest that this was not so. First, there
is the Sermon on the Plain (6.20–49), meant specifically for disciples
(v. 20). Scholars have puzzled for a long time over the literary relationship between this and the better-known and much longer Sermon on
the Mount (Matt. 5–7). Broadly speaking, those who think that Luke
used Matthew's Gospel hold that the Sermon on the Plain represents
part of Luke's rewriting and rearrangement of Matthew; for example,
on this view, he shortened the first beatitude to 'How blest are the poor',
leaving out 'in spirit'. A greater number of scholars think that Luke and
Matthew used the same source, each making some changes of his own.
Whichever view is adopted, it means that, as almost always in the
Gospels, the teaching of Jesus comes to us through the filter of the early
churches, who selected, adapted and expanded it. To argue that this
diminishes its authority would be to imply that the Holy Spirit sus-
pended operations after the resurrection. The New Testament is the
product of the church in its most inspired, creative and formative
period; Christ is the living reality behind it, and that gives to the gospels
as artistic wholes an authority peculiarly their own. In the context of
those affirmations we can be content to leave a little blurred, sometimes
at least, the distinction between the teaching of Jesus himself and the
reflections of the first Christians upon that teaching.

What, then, are the main themes of Luke's sermon? It begins, like
Matthew's, with some beatitudes, only fewer in number and more terse
in expression than Matthew's. The poor, the hungry, the sorrowful and
Christians who are persecuted are declared happy and, conversely, woes
are pronounced on the rich, the full, the scoffers – the real meaning of
'laugh' in v. 25 – and those of whom everyone speaks well (vv. 20–26).
These verses perhaps appear to support the view that Christians are
miserable killjoys bent on 'pie in the sky', but this would be mistaken.
The Old Testament background of some of these words,[5] and the New
Testament as a whole, suggests a different picture. True disciples are
those who have little to rely on or to call their own or, if they have, sit
lightly to it ('poor in spirit'); they feel acutely the broken, imperfect
nature of human life and of their own in particular; they bear some-

thing of the weight of the world's evil with more sorrow than anger, and suffer, for the sake of Christ, the consequences of being out of step with the powers and authorities of their day. Such people might seem to be simply the flotsam and jetsam of the world, but the teaching which follows shows that, on the contrary, so far from being benighted and forlorn, they will find the resources for loving to a quite remarkable extent (vv. 27–36), and find themselves the possessors of the peace, inner freedom and wealth which come from God (vv. 37f.).

The Sermon on the Plain shows that real goodness runs deep. Sitting lightly to what one has, living prayerfully ('those who hunger'), vulnerably and generously, issues inevitably in a striking gentleness towards other people (vv. 41f.). But this, like all the other expressions of discipleship, is not a cosmetic facade hiding what is really in the depths of the heart, but rather the spontaneous overflow of the disciple's true self (vv. 43–45). The standard might be breathtaking, but Luke has placed this teaching almost immediately after the appointment of the apostles. For them, therefore, there can be no 'power game'; they may not throw their ecclesiastical weight around, for, 'A pupil is not superior to his teacher; but everyone, when his training is complete, will reach his teacher's level' (v. 40). (Luke 17.7–10 shows that this cannot mean an equality of status with Christ.)

Two other passages should be noted here. In this Gospel Jesus sends his disciples out, not on one mission, as in Mark and Matthew, but on two (9.1–6; 10.1–12). The number of the disciples in each narrative – twelve and seventy or seventy-two[6] respectively – has often been thought to symbolize the fact that first Jew and then Gentile will be the privileged recipients of the healing work done by the agents of Christ. There are difficulties with this view, not least the fact that the sphere of operations here is still Palestine! However that may be, some verses at the end of the second mission indicate (10.17–20) that the disciples themselves are the most privileged group of all, not so much because they have been given the power to defeat evil ('snakes and scorpions'), but because God himself has acknowledged them. And since he is among them as one who serves (22.27), the power of love rather than the love of power will be the hallmark of those who serve him.

The extent of God's service to the human race Luke has yet to make clear. Simeon's words to Mary, as we saw, gave a hint of what was to come, the temptation narrative ended ominously, and Jesus' ministry from the very beginning was embroiled in controversy and conflict (Luke 4 and 5). But from Luke 9 onwards it is made more clear that the fulfilment of what God intends will come about only through suffering and death. In words taken, with only slight changes, from Mark, the keystone of God's plan is described:

> The Son of Man has to undergo great sufferings, and to be rejected by the elders, chief priests, and doctors of the law, to be put to death and to be raised again on the third day (9.22).

Although a vindication beyond death is briefly mentioned here, the transfiguration which follows (vv. 28–36) declares more fully that the divine *imprimatur* overshadows even the darkest episodes of the future.

So Luke began to trace the progress of Jesus to Jerusalem. In his view the beginning of the journey was a moment of destiny, and so he described it in appropriately solemn language (9.51).

It is impossible to trace the route which Jesus and his disciples took to Jerusalem. (Luke was not particularly interested in geographical details, as the oddness of the reference in 17.11 suggests.) What mattered was that they made the journey. And so from time to time throughout the long middle section of his Gospel (9.51–18.14),[7] Luke reminded his readers that Jesus and his disciples were proceeding inexorably towards Jerusalem. These reminders heighten the growing tension, for the reader already knows that the final conflict and fulfilment are to be expected there (9.31; 13.33). But before we come to that, we must look more fully at Luke's portrait of Jesus and his message.

# - 3 -

# The Way of the Messiah

In this chapter it will not always be easy to discern the emphases and concerns which are distinctive to Luke. Where Luke followed Mark we can form some idea of the extent of his own contribution by simply comparing his account with Mark's. In the long central section of his Gospel (9.51–18.14) we do not know for certain the original wording of his sources unless, of course, we take the view that he used Matthew's Gospel. So scholars differ widely over the question of how much in these chapters is Luke's own work. At one extreme there are those who, like Drury and Goulder, argue that Luke composed a great deal of them himself; at the other, there are those, like Marshall, who think that Luke followed his sources fairly carefully.

Whatever the truth of the matter may be, we can be fairly certain that Luke wrote the 'connecting bits', such as 'Jesus said to his disciples', and this allows us to make a broad distinction between teaching intended primarily for disciples (e.g. 12.22–34) and teaching for the people at large (e.g. 12.54–56). The former will be discussed in sections i and ii, the latter in section iii. But first we shall look briefly at one or two distinctive features of Luke's portrait of Jesus.

Luke made it very clear from the beginning that Jesus would occupy the centre of the stage. John the Baptist bows out before Jesus' ministry even begins (3.19f.), and his death at the hands of Herod is noted in no more than three words (9.9). In Mark the vocation of Jesus is to proclaim the kingdom, whereas in Luke Jesus announces, in his first sermon at least (4.16–30), not the kingdom, but himself. (John's Gospel deals more fully with this paradox or contradiction, pointing out that God and Jesus witness to each other: 5.31f.; 8.13–18.) Luke continued to use the traditional phrase 'kingdom of God', but the overall impression of his writings shows that he could envisage no message other than Jesus himself.

Luke's devotion to and reverence for Jesus can be seen in some of the small but significant alterations he made to the narrative of Mark. In his Gospel people usually follow, rather than accompany, Jesus. Although Luke wrote that great crowds 'accompanied' Jesus at one point (14.25), the fact that Jesus turned to address them shows that the evangelist pictured him out in front. Again, people in Luke address Jesus more respectfully (compare, for example, the words of the disciples in Mark 4.38 and Luke 8.24); sometimes, it seems, he must not even share a verb with other people.[1] But that is not all. There is no suggestion in Luke's Gospel that Jesus' knowledge or power were limited in any way; any sayings or details in Mark implying that they were (e.g. Mark 6.5; 13.32) are omitted.

By these and other details we gain an impression of how Luke pictured Jesus. For him Jesus was a man of supreme self-composure, authority and dignity, always master of a situation, always taking the initiative. His extraordinary power and uncanny insight were to be expected in one who was a man of the Spirit – a point which Luke emphasized strongly in chapters 3 and 4. Another gift of the Spirit was wisdom (as Acts 6.10 implies), and so one of the main themes of Luke's portrait is that of 'Jesus, prophet and teacher'.

We have seen that the evangelist deliberately evoked memories of Elijah and Elisha by the way he wrote up certain stories, but the 'prophet' theme emerges at other points, too. It seems clear from Acts that an Old Testament prediction strongly influenced Luke here: 'The Lord your God will raise up a prophet from among you like myself, and you shall listen to him' (Deut. 18.15; Acts 3.22; 7.37). So a verse in the last chapter of his Gospel probably reflects the evangelist's view of Jesus: '. . . a prophet powerful in speech and action before God and the whole people' (24.19). This is not to deny that Luke also believed that Jesus was Son of God, Lord and Saviour, but we are concentrating here on an aspect of Jesus' life and ministry which is given particular prominence in this Gospel.

This characteristic was first foreshadowed in the passage about his boyhood (2.41–52). The existence of many similar stories about other great figures of the ancient world, including Moses and Alexander the Great, suggests that this one is a legend. This does not mean that it is valueless; we should ask, rather, what Luke was trying to say through it. In this case the story invites the reader to see that the wisdom of Jesus was unprecedented, drawing from those who were deeply read in the wisdom of the past, but already promising to go far beyond even that (vv. 46f.). And yet this was no twelve-year-old prodigy, Palestine's answer, as it were, to a young musical genius of today. In words implying a remarkable closeness to God, the boy Jesus speaks of 'my Father', thus indicating that his wisdom is the gift of God. With that in mind we turn now to a consideration of some of the major themes of Jesus' teaching as presented by Luke.

(i) The cost of discipleship

There has been a tendency to think of the Third Evangelist as a genial family doctor who spiced his Gospel with all the best stories, such as the nativity story, the Good Samaritan and the Prodigal Son. But his writings also contain some of the most demanding sayings and harshest stories in the entire New Testament. One such saying comes at the very beginning of Jesus' journey to Jerusalem. Since the chronology of each Gospel is to some extent the writer's own,[2] we may be sure that Luke placed it there deliberately, as if to say to his readers, 'This is what it is all about'. He described three would-be disciples (9.57–62), to all of whom Jesus gives chilling answers. The most severe of all is given to the second man, who asks permission to bury his father first: 'Leave the dead to bury their dead' (v. 60). Such an idea was abhorrent to most races of the ancient world, and not least to Jews, since burying the dead was regarded as a most sacred obligation. Not only that, it ran contrary even to what was taught in the early churches about care for one's relatives, as I Tim. 5.8 indicates.[3] The presence of this saying in both Luke and Matthew (Matt. 8.22) is striking evidence that the first Christians, when adapting the teaching of Jesus, did not simply rewrite it to suit themselves.

The point of Jesus' reply to the third candidate for discipleship ('No one who sets his hand to the plough and then keeps looking back is fit for the kingdom of God,' v. 62), lies in its contrast with an Old Testament story. Elijah, unlike Jesus here, gave Elisha permission to say farewell to his parents (I Kings 19.20) before taking up his apprenticeship as a prophet. Thus Luke makes clear what an aspiring disciple faces: a demand unprecedented in its urgency and its extent, ferreting people out of comfortable bolt-holes and established roles (v. 58), and going deeper even than the most sacred ties.

The same note recurs in chapters 12 and 14. It is likely that Luke

lived at a time when the still relatively new faith was dividing families
and households.

> For from now on, five members of a family will be divided, three
> against two and two against three; father against son and son against
> father, mother against daughter and daughter against mother, mother
> against son's wife and son's wife against mother-in-law (12.53).

A comparison with Matthew 10.35, where the same saying occurs, suggests that Luke adapted the words which he found in his source to show
that this was the state of affairs one might now expect in the time of the
church. If this was indeed the background against which he was writing,
it would explain why he retained the more Hebraic form of the saying
which Matthew also has (10.37); Matthew, conscious perhaps of the
fifth commandment, wrote down, 'No man is worthy of me who cares
more for father or mother than for me'; Luke was content to include
this teaching in all its original austerity: 'If anyone comes to me and
does not hate his father and mother . . . he cannot be a disciple of mine'
(14.26).

These verses sound strange and offensive in societies where most
members of churches are the children of those who were church members before them, and who are more at home with family services and
the like. All the more reason why the stringency of this Gospel is
needed to avoid an indictment similar to that of Kierkegaard against the
Danish church of the early nineteenth century: 'They have changed
Christianity and made it too much of a consolation and forgotten it's a
demand.'

The claims of discipleship go deepest of all. That is the clear message
of these verses. They are not, of course, irreconcilable with the fifth
commandment, for if a disciple cannot love members of his own house-
hold, how may he love the neighbour whom he chances to meet (Luke
10.25–37)?

But there is another austere theme running through Luke's Gospel.
The evangelist was anxious to show that becoming a follower of Jesus
meant leaving everything. To the story of Levi's call (5.27–32), which
he found in Mark, he added the phrase 'left everything behind' (v. 32).
Earlier in the chapter the same was said of the disciples present at the
miraculous catch of fish (5.1–11). This cost of discipleship is expressed
most searchingly of all in chapter 14: 'So also none of you can be a
disciple of mine without parting with all his possessions' (v. 33).

We must pause here and consider this verse more fully, particularly the question of whether Luke understood it literally. A survey of Luke-Acts as a whole shows that he did not. Zacchaeus did not give up everything (19.8); some women healed by Jesus ministered to him and his disciples 'out of their own resources' (8.3); and although the 'Christian communism' of Acts 2 and 4 should not be forgotten (on this see Chapter 4), there are other Christians in Acts, such as Philip (21.8), who had houses of their own. And so 14.33 should probably be understood in the same way as the earlier v. 26: the claims of discipleship come not only before relationships, but also before possessions.

The amount of material in Luke-Acts about wealth and poverty suggests that Luke knew of a church, or probably several, which included both very rich and very poor people. (On this, see also Chapter 6.) It is impossible to do justice to all the relevant passages here, but we may note three parables, all of which are in the middle section of the Gospel. The first, the parable of the rich fool (12.13–21), the evangelist deliberately placed immediately before the teaching on carefreeness (discussed below). It anticipates the theme of that section that life is a gift. The wording of v. 20 implies that it is not only a gift, but also a loan from God. A more literal translation would be: 'You fool, this very night they (perhaps God's angel of death) will ask for the return of your life.'

The other two parables comprise most of chapter 16: the parable of the Unjust Steward (vv. 1–13), and the story of Lazarus and the Rich Man (vv. 19–31). The first is notoriously difficult and was probably felt to be so very soon after Jesus' own lifetime. To discover its original meaning, vv. 9–13 must momentarily be set aside. In Chapter 1, I pointed out how the early Christians used the teaching of Jesus, adapting and expanding it where they felt it necessary to do so. C. H. Dodd suggested that vv. 9–13 consist of texts for three different sermons based on the parable.[4] And so although they are important both in themselves and as lessons which the early churches drew from the parable, they do not necessarily provide the clue to its original meaning.

Recently, however, a new interpretation has been suggested,[5] which solves the problem of Jesus apparently commending dishonest conduct. On this view, the steward's accounts originally included the interest on the debts. But the charging of interest was against the law of God (e.g. Psalm 15.5), although ways round this were found. The steward, therefore, removed from the debtors' bills the interest which was due, thereby acting virtuously and winning the commendation of his master, and no doubt of Jesus too. On this interpretation 'the lord' in v. 8 could

be either Jesus or the employer of the story. The loss of revenue to his
employer would be amply compensated by his enhanced public reputation, a vitally important matter to any member of the society in which
Jesus lived. And so this parable, too, is about the right use of money,
especially in a crisis.

The parable of the Rich Man and Lazarus (16.19–31) is almost certainly an adaptation, whether by Jesus himself or someone else, of a
popular folk-tale. Luke may have intended a contrast with the previous
parable ('This is how not to use your money'), and a sequel to v. 17, if
that verse is not ironical, with its emphasis on the law and the prophets.
In other words, the Old Testament already makes clear how a man
should use his wealth. If he takes no notice of it, a miracle will make no
impression on him either (v. 31). So the parable reflects the view,
almost certainly held by Luke, that someone who is unfaithful to his
own religious tradition will not readily respond to the gospel.

So Luke, more than any other New Testament writer, stressed the
cost of discipleship. In so doing he did not have in mind a demand
which could be met at a stroke. The sacrifices necessary were not the
product of a sudden enthusiasm; in that case they would be comparable
to seed sprouting up with no root (8.13). Rather, they followed a careful
consideration of the cost (14.28–32), and were a permanent feature of
the disciple's pilgrimage. Only this Gospel reminds its readers that
taking up the cross is a daily task (9.23; contrast Mark 8.34), for which
the Christian wayfarer must ask God for daily provision (11.3, contrast
Matthew 6.11). Typical also of Luke is his ending to the parable of the
sower. Although Matthew and Mark also have the parable, only he
emphasizes perseverence: 'the seed in good soil represents those who
. . . by their perseverance yield a harvest' (8.15).

Is the disciple, then, left with anything? The paradoxical answer,
according to both Luke and other New Testament writers, is 'nothing
and everything'.


(ii)  The generosity of God

So far we have found much in this Gospel about the cost of discipleship.
These stupendous demands, Luke seems to be saying, are also part of
the divine plan. The natural reaction of most people to such demands
is enunciated in the Gospel itself: 'Then who can be saved?' (18.26).
This question comes in the story of the rich man, which Luke was
probably glad to borrow from Mark because it demonstrated once more

the deeper, more personal kind of giving required of the disciple of Christ: 'Sell everything you have and distribute to the poor' (v. 22). But the story ends not on a note of despair, 'Who can be saved?', but on one of hope: 'What is impossible for men is possible for God' (v. 27), which might perhaps be paraphrased as 'Let God take care of that'. In short, Jesus taught that God was not only more demanding than people cared to think, but also more generous than they dared to hope. And so we turn from the theme of the demands of God to that of his generosity and of living by grace.

The last phrase, admittedly, is a much-used piece of Christian jargon, and yet it describes the essence of discipleship: when God's undeserved goodness becomes the chief means of understanding and interpreting life, and the creative centre of a person's own life, then he or she 'lives by grace'.

It is impossible to survey adequately all the material here, but we shall examine some of the relevant passages under three heads. First, a person may experience God's generosity as forgiveness. The famous parable of the Prodigal Son would be better named the parable of the Loving Father (15.11–32), if only because the second half of the story was originally as important as the first half. Luke either knew or guessed that what occasioned a parable like this was the controversial, or rather scandalous, visits of Jesus to the homes of people like Levi (5.27–32) and Zacchaeus (19.1–10), quislings and cheats as they usually were. The parable illustrates both the generosity of God and the offence taken at that generosity by the person who believes, or chooses to believe, that God runs the world on a merit-mark system. What must have given the story much greater force was the fact that Jesus practised what he preached. The medium was the message, and the conjunction of action (15.2) and parable were an example, to the disciples at least, of how Jesus demonstrated the generosity of God. Even repentance (i.e. change of heart or outlook) is not a merit by which one may qualify for that generosity, for, as the story of Zacchaeus shows, repentance itself is created by grace.[6] The same crucial point was made earlier in Luke's Gospel: 'her great love proves that her many sins have been forgiven' (7.47a).

Secondly, the generosity of God may be encountered through prayer. (On this subject there are several parables which occur in this Gospel only.) The story of the Pharisee and the Publican (18.9–14) may have been included because Luke wished to counter 'holier than thou' attitudes in the churches he knew. The Pharisee was indulging in

self-congratulation, rather than praying; by contrast, the Publican illustrates how only the person who recognizes he has no claims upon God
is in a position to be surprised by his generosity.

Another parable offers a colourful picture of a man whose repeated
hammering at the door finally compels his exasperated neighbour to
get out of bed and give him the bread he needed (11.5–8). Like the story
of the Unjust Judge (18.1–8), it was intended to illustrate 'how much
more' God will give his children what they need. It is possible, however, that the end of v. 8 should be translated rather differently from the
way it usually is and read, 'yet a concern for his own reputation will
make him get up and give him all he needs'. In other words, God has a
reputation to keep up!

It would be easy, but mistaken, to deduce from the verses which
follow, 'And so I say to you, ask and you will receive . . .' (vv. 9–13),
that prayer is a blank cheque which God is bound to honour. The basic
message is not in doubt: God is only too ready to give good gifts to men,
but what are these good things? A new car, promotion (as some modern
religious sects teach)? And what did Jesus originally say God would
give? 'Good gifts' (Matt. 7–11)? 'The Holy Spirit' (Luke 11.13)? 'A
good spirit' (one important manuscript has this reading)? We cannot
be certain, but Luke's version should probably be regarded as an
inspired interpretation of the original: it is a question of going to God
with the right attitude. 'Ask for the big things, and the little things will
take care of themselves,' was the advice of Origen, in the third century.

Does the Gospel then teach that asking God for material things is
out of place? It would seem rash to say 'yes' in the light of the Lord's
Prayer, with its petition 'Give us each day our daily bread' (11.3). There
may, however, be a connection in thought here with the story of the
manna in the desert (Ex. 16), which is described in Psalm 78.24 as 'the
bread of heaven' and in I Cor. 10.3 as 'spiritual food'. The prayer may
therefore mean 'Give us each day a foretaste of the life of the world to
come.'

More light on the question of what the disciple should ask God for
comes from the passage about freedom from care: ' "Therefore," he
said to his disciples, "I bid you put away anxious thought about food
to keep you alive . . ." ' (12.22–34). There can be few passages of the
New Testament whose difficulties are underestimated as much as this
one, or which attract so many unrealistically sentimental ideas. (Although Luke does not have 'Take no thought for the morrow' – Matt.
6.34 – he does have 'Think of the lilies': v. 27.) Are these words to be

taken at face value and understood as guaranteeing the Christian's bread supply? In the light of history and of contemporary realities it would be wrong to answer glibly in the affirmative. There are no doubt many Christians in Africa and India with insufficient to eat. However, the picture of the early churches in Acts (e.g. 4.34f.; 11.28–30) and the epistles of Paul (e.g. Rom. 15.26) show from which source the needy Christian's bread supply should really come, and that is from those Christians who are better-off. If their lack of generosity makes it impossible for their starving brother to believe the teaching of the gospel, the stern words of 'causes of stumbling' are especially applicable to them: it would be better for them to be thrown into the sea . . . (17.1f.).

Neither here, nor anywhere else in the Gospel, is there the slightest hint that God is oblivious to man's physical needs. In fact the passage on freedom from care brings us to the third facet of the theme of this section: the generosity of God in creation. Luke was careful to say that these words were addressed to disciples only (v. 22), not because God cares only for them, but because only they may be expected to find the secret of freedom from anxiety: life, with all its blessings, and the life of God, with all its wealth (vv. 32–34), are free gifts to be received thankfully and trustingly. This is the proper basis of human life, and therefore of discipleship.

The demand and the gift of the gospel, indivisible as they are, find expression in vv. 31f., 'set your mind upon his kingdom', for that is what really matters, and it can be done gladly, because, though costing everything, true life is still a free gift (v. 32). So the cost of discipleship and the generosity of God are brought together, and indeed must go together. The demands of the gospel, by themselves, invite only despair or cynicism; but apart from them the generosity of God would be distorted into grace 'on the cheap'.

A disciple, therefore, is one who has been surprised by the generosity of God and thus enabled to respond to his demands. Consequently, such a person will be generous to others in uncalculating forgiveness (17.3f.), in almsgiving (12.33) and unstinting kindness (10.25–34). To calculate, of course, would be to warp the quality of love, and yet he can be sure that such actions are what really count with God (14.12–14; compare Matt. 25.31–46). But however much he does, he will never have done more than his duty. He remains in God's debt (17.7–10), and humility, the product of being more aware of God than himself, will be the hallmark of his everyday life (18.9–14; 14.7–11). Such conduct must be no mere 'flash in the pan', a frequent emphasis of Luke, for history's grand

finale is still a way off, and the disciple meantime must make the most
of what God has entrusted to him (19.11–27). That will be a matter,
not of words, but of obedience to *the* Word (6.47–49; 11.27f.). Indeed,
only if 'the Lord's word' is heard over and over again can a life of
obedient service be sustained (10.38–42). (There is a hint here, perhaps,
in this story of Martha and Mary of another tension in Luke's church;
'doers' in God's cause can't really be 'doers' until they have first learned
the discipline and therapy of simply 'being' before God.)

We have already seen how Luke portrayed the Christian life as something of a pilgrim's progress. But he was well aware that regression,
whether through sheer neglect (11.24–26) or cynicism (12.41–46), was a
constant possibility. Right to the end, the disciple must presume
nothing. It is only human to want to know whether one has finally
'arrived', but no such certainty can be offered. No one can ever be said
to have salvation 'in the bag'. That perhaps is the implication of the
enigmatic v. 37 at the end of the section on 'The Day of the Son of
Man' (17.22–37). And so, although there will be 'false alarms' before
the end of everything (vv. 22f.), the disciple must be on the alert, not
losing sight of the penultimate nature of most human activity (vv. 27f.;
compare Paul's teaching in I Cor. 7.29–31). Finally, to the servant who
remains alert there is held out the prospect at the end of that which
inspired and made possible his discipleship in the first place – God's
ministry to him (12.37). Luke made it clear early on in his Gospel
(4.16–30) that this ministry was to be enacted in Jesus and mediated to
people through him. That remained the pattern to the very end: 'Yet
here am I among you like a servant' (22.27).

## (iii) Conflict

The impressionistic sketch given in the last section, of the Christian
life according to Luke, was drawn from the blocks of teaching which the
evangelist understood to be for disciples. In other sections, however,
Jesus is portrayed as uttering dire warnings to his fellow countrymen,
and we must now consider the significance of these, together with the
reasons for opposition to Jesus during his ministry. As we do so, it will
be necessary to retrace our steps a little, since accounts of conflict and
controversy occur early in the Gospels of both Mark and Luke. Such
incidents may have taken place at an early stage of Jesus' ministry, but
Luke's arrangement of them is not chronological, as some of the alterations he makes to Mark's account show. The settings, also, may not be

original. For example, Luke may have supplied the kind of question or the kind of situation which he thought suitable for the miracles or sayings of Jesus. But whether the precise details are accurate or not, there are good reasons for thinking that the overall picture reflects the issues and grounds of conflict which developed during his ministry.

More than any of the other evangelists, Luke portrayed Jesus as a prophet. He also included in his Gospel a rather cryptic saying which suggests that Jesus regarded himself as a prophet:

> Today and tomorrow I shall be casting out devils and working cures; on the third day I reach my goal. However, I must be on my way today and tomorrow and the next day, because it is unthinkable for a prophet to meet his death anywhere but in Jerusalem (13.32f.).

Like most of the prophets of the Old Testament, Jesus incurred the opposition of his compatriots. He issued, as they did, a summons to repentance, and, like many of them, announced God's offer of salvation. He may have believed that the end of the world was near, and that his contemporaries must prepare for it. He may have hoped for a national reformation. But we can be sure that he felt his vocation was to proclaim, by word and deed, the kingdom of God, and that he encountered considerable opposition. Even in Galilee the response was poor (10.13f.), but it was typical of the nation as a whole (11.29–32). In these passages Jesus' contemporaries are compared with well-known – in some cases, notorious – people from the Old Testament. We must therefore consider briefly what were the reasons, according to Luke, for the opposition and apparent blindness of many of the Jews.

The society into which Jesus was born was a turbulent one. Most Jews had never acquiesced in the Roman occupation of their country, and their understanding of their religion encouraged them in the view that this state of affairs was intolerable. Zealots constituted the guerrilla groups who were prepared to use force in the cause of national freedom. Pharisees believed that pressure on God in the form of fasting, prayers, and, above all, obedience to the Law, was the way to national salvation. It is possible that the original form of the answer to the Pharisees' question, 'When will the kingdom of God come?', was something like, 'Observation of the Law will not make the kingdom come' (17.20f.).

As well as Zealots and Pharisees, scribes, who had become indispensable biblical consultants in the mammoth task of applying the Law to every part of life, were also influential. So, too, were the Sadducees, a more shadowy Jerusalem-based group who believed in the Law of

Moses and, it would seem, little else (Luke 20.27; Acts 23.8). Of these groups the Pharisees and scribes probably spear-headed the opposition to Jesus, who almost certainly alienated Zealots and Sadducees as well, but references in the Gospels to these sects are very few.

Jesus and his opponents differed sharply on issues which both he and they believed were fundamental. He believed that his rehabilitation of characters such as Zacchaeus reflected God's creative generosity; they looked upon it as 'letting the side down' to the point of national betrayal and religious apostasy. He rejected as a burden, rather than a means to life (11.45–52), the 'small print' (or rather, the unwritten equivalent of 'small print') which scribes had added in profusion to the scriptures; they took the view that it was as important as scripture itself. Jesus' rapport with God enabled him to mediate the divine forgiveness (5.17–26);[7] such personal, charismatic authority in the eyes of scribes and Pharisees amounted to nothing less than blasphemy. Finally, Jesus and his opponents differed on the question of what keeping the sabbath as a sacred day involved; his own more positive, humanitarian approach (6.1–11, 13; 10.7; 14.1–6) incurred still more hostility, precisely because it raised a plethora of searching questions. What was the real nature and purpose of God? What authority did the unwritten rules of conventional religion have? What was the basis for the authority of Jesus?

The most common accusation made against the opponents of Jesus in the Gospels, whether explicitly or implicitly, is that of blindness. Of course, the controversies and conflicts in which the early churches were engaged, particularly with Jews, may have been read back to some extent into the ministry of Jesus. But from Luke's standpoint such opposition, whether then or later, was basically the same. At the very end of his two-volume work he quoted at some length a prophecy of Isaiah which he would have found in Mark's third chapter, and which, it seems, he kept back in order to make it part of the 'coda' to his work. Significantly, it includes a description of a people's failure to see: 'You may look and look, but you will never see. For this people's mind has become gross . . . and their eyes are closed' (Acts 28.26f.).

The inability to see properly was partly a failure in perspective; external correctness and attention to religious minutiae cannot be substitutes for deeper, more inward failures (11.37–44). These strictures were directed against the Pharisees, but it is worth noting that one of the distinctive, though puzzling, features of Luke-Acts is the number of favourable references to Pharisees.[8] Significantly, perhaps, Luke did not make those who accused Jesus of collusion with the devil either scribes (like Mark) or Pharisees (like Matthew). In this passage (11.14–23) the anonymous objectors refuse to recognize the goodness of what is happening before their eyes. Blindness here is the result of prejudice and was expressed in the request for a sign (v. 16), a request which the Gospels always condemn.

But what was so wrong in asking for a sign? There are echoes here of Old Testament stories, such as Ex. 16.2f.; 17.2. In both cases the request, or complaint, amounted to a demand that God should prove himself, and that meant that they were holding back from the way of faith and obedience. But was it not reasonable, it may be asked, to have something to go on? Blind faith, after all, is hardly desirable. But the Gospels are unanimous in saying that there was enough to 'go on' in the ministry of Jesus. Only John's Gospel calls his miracles 'signs', but the other Gospels imply that that is what they were, for what else but the power of God could lie behind the cures performed by Jesus (11.14–23)? 'If it is by the finger of God that I drive out the devils, then be sure the kingdom of God has already come upon you' (v. 20).

Jesus' contemporaries, with few exceptions, were not only blind to what was going on in the ministry of Jesus; they also failed to discern that it was the eleventh hour for their nation. How absurd to be able to predict the weather and not to discern God's hour when it struck (12.54–56)! And why point an accusing finger at others when time was running out for everyone (13.1–9)? The nation had lost its way, but if it had discerned the real 'drift' of the Old Testament, it would have understood its vocation in the world very differently.

With this theme of judgment upon Jesus' compatriots, we are brought back to a recurring concern of Luke. At the very end of his work the response of others is contrasted sharply with that of the Jews: 'The Gentiles will listen' (Acts 28.28). Again, their own scriptures are used in evidence against them. Elijah and Elisha ministered to Gentiles (4.25–27), Solomon and Jonah taught or preached to Gentiles (11.29–32). All the more reason why the bounds of Judaism should be transcended, for 'what is there is greater than Jonah' (v. 32).

The apparent anti-Jewishness of Luke in retaining or writing up these passages may seem alien and even offensive to the twentieth century. Yet the church must always hear these words addressed to herself. The response of the unbelieving Jews in Luke-Acts is that of those who have come to take God for granted, or fail to see that he is less conventional, more disturbing and more generous than they. It is the response of those who live with fixed ideas about God, instead of recognizing that the life of faith is both a gift and an inquiry, a process of receiving and exploring in which humility is indispensable.

A man spoke and acted in the name of God and invited his contemporaries to throw in their lot with him. The movement he started no doubt seemed insignificant like a mustard seed (13.18f.), unnoticed at first like leaven (13.20f.), even undignified and unworthy, like an invitation to a party with people who are 'not your sort' (14.15–24). But in spite of appearances the message was clear: 'The kingdom of God is among you' (17.21).

(iv) In Jerusalem

Both before and since King David made Jerusalem his capital, many myths had grown up about the city. It was the centre of the earth, and the site of Zion, the mountain of God, and so in a special sense the place where God and man met. Thus it is not surprising that Jerusalem had a particular importance for Luke. It was the place where God's promises were to be fulfilled, and from which a new beginning was to be made. But the city had its dark side, too. Jerusalem was where prophets were all too likely to meet their deaths (13.33), and the city which recognized neither her hour of destiny nor the source of her true well-being (13.34f.; 19.42–44). That is why her days were numbered, and why (only in this Gospel) Christ wept over her (19.41).

For all these reasons the entry of Jesus into Jerusalem has a special poignancy in Luke. There is, however, a historical difficulty about this incident (19.28–38). Would not Jesus have been arrested for being the centre of a dangerous Messianic demonstration (vv. 37f., although the words of the disciples here sound much less political than in Mark's version)? It is not likely that Jesus' popular support would have been so great as to deter the authorities, and so it is probable that here we have a mixture of history and legend. For example, the evangelists credited Jesus with supernatural knowledge about the ass, although the animal was almost certainly borrowed in a way quite natural and normal in Jewish society. (It is all too easily forgotten that the title 'son of God' was and is a way of describing Jesus' oneness with God in love and obedience; it did not mean that he was omniscient and omnipotent.) In other words, the Gospel writers overlaid what actually happened with what they thought it meant. Here the message is clear: the king has 'entered his own realm, and his own would not receive him' (John 1.11). Their refusal to submit to judgment sealed their own destruction.[9]

These themes are elaborated in the rabbinic-sounding question-and-answer sessions which follow (20.1–45). Most of them may well be historical, even if the hand of the evangelist, as always, can be discerned from time to time. What are the points at issue here? The first controversy, and the parable which follows (vv. 1–19), deals with the authority of Jesus. His refusal to answer his opponents' questions about his authority because they would not answer his about John's baptism was not as evasive as it might appear. The authority of John and that of Jesus, although very different, went hand in hand; if people would not stand up and be counted in support of John they were hardly likely to side with Jesus. As for the Parable of the Wicked Husbandmen, a true-to-life story,[10] we have grown accustomed to identify Jesus with 'the son' (v. 13), as indeed Luke did, but Jesus' listeners may not have done so, and in any case, as I have noted, 'son of God' did not necessarily imply divinity.[11] The emphasis in the story rests not so much on the identity of Jesus, but on the culpability of those who will not face up to what they owe to God.

Little comment is needed on the reply to the question about tribute: 'Pay Caesar what is due to Caesar, and pay God what is due to God' (v. 25). It contains in a nutshell the tension of the Christian in society, and is one of several verses in the Gospels which indicate that Jesus was not a zealot.

The last two questions provide a fitting prelude to what is to come. Rabbis were used to dealing with what were called 'mocking questions', like that of the Sadducees about the resurrection (27.40) and the hypothetical woman who outlived seven husbands. Jesus swept aside their sophistry by firmly asserting what Old Testament writers had groped after, that the relationship God established with people in this life did not end with death (v. 38). And what better sequel to this could there be than the question of God's final vindication of Jesus (vv. 41–44)? The question itself, put here by Jesus, 'How can they say that the Messiah is son of David? . . . David calls him "Lord"; how then can he be David's son?' (vv. 41, 44), sounds more ambiguous in the Greek, and many scholars question whether Jesus would have asked it. But as Luke and the other two synoptists narrated it, the story was an unmistakable pointer to the resurrection by which alone God's Messiah, after being David's son on earth, might be exalted to become his Lord.

The story of the widow's mite (21.1–4) affords a striking contrast with the shallow piety of the religious leaders who have questioned Jesus. But there may be a deeper meaning here. The phrase translated in v. 4, and in its parallel Mark 12.44, by 'all she had to live on' could also mean 'her whole life'. Thus it is not impossible that the evangelists interpreted the story as a parable of Jesus' own sacrifice. Out of apparent poverty (compare II Cor. 8.9), he gave far more than all the Sadducees and scribes put together.

The remainder of chapter 21 is full of difficulties for the modern reader unable to accept it literally. Its significance becomes clearer in the light of the last chapters of the Gospel. As Luke had already intimated, the end will not come immediately; instead the disciples face a long, hard road, and they should not be fooled into thinking otherwise (vv. 8–11). In this long interim period there will be disasters (v. 11) and persecutions (vv. 12–17), and, almost as if history were repeating itself (for Luke's language here echoes the Old Testament), Jerusalem will pay the price for her blindness (vv. 20–24). In spite of all this they should not imagine that the world is hopeless or God-forsaken; their ultimate well-being is assured (v. 18), and the last word, they may be certain, rests with God (vv. 25–28). More precisely it will finally become clear, even if the very 'fabric of the universe' (Marshall, p. 775) seems to be breaking up, that the key to history and the ultimate meaning of everything lie with one marked by suffering and sacrifice (v. 27). This chapter, therefore, asserts, in contemporary terms, that whatever may happen in the future, the abiding reality is Christ, and for that reason his followers must 'be on the alert' (v. 36). This cannot mean watching anxiously for signs of the end (as Acts 1.7 shows), but rather persevering in the way of the Messiah (vv. 34–36). And that, according to the New Testament, means living for the time being (however long that may be) in faith, hope and love.

Apart from the symbolism of vv. 25–27, a difficulty remains with the passage about the signs of the end (vv. 25–33). Verse 32, 'this generation will live to see it all', implies that the end will come within the lifetime of the first disciples. A paraphrase might indicate the meaning Luke attached to this saying: 'This generation will witness the dawn of the last age of history'.

So far in this section most of the passages we have discussed can be found also in Mark. The so-called 'apocalyptic'[12] chapter 21 consists of Luke's rewriting, with some additions and omissions, of Mark 13 in order to emphasize the qualities the disciples of Christ will need in the long period which lies before them. This sombre yet confident discourse leads naturally into Luke's account of the last hours of Jesus' life, and to its distinctive features we now turn.

First, Luke made it plain that even crucifixion is part of the divine plan: 'The Son of Man is going his appointed way' (22.22), a way which includes being counted as a bandit, for that, too, was foreshadowed in the Old Testament (22.37; Isa. 53.12). His opponents' moment of triumph, it is implied, is theirs only by divine concession (22.53). As usual, chapters 22 and 23 contain a mixture of history and comment. Old Testament allusions, especially, reinforce the impression that from first to last this was the work of God (as Paul wrote to the Corinthians, II Cor. 5.18a).

Several distinctive touches mark Luke's portrait of Jesus in these chapters. A certain gentleness towards the disciples, and especially towards Peter, is shown (22.31–34). The high priest's servant, attacked by a disciple in Gethsemane, is healed (22.51). Jesus is portrayed as more concerned for his compatriots than for himself (23.26–32). At the very end he prays for forgiveness for his tormentors (23.34),[13] and extends the hope of resurrection to a thief (23.43). Perhaps we should include here, although this judgment is more subjective, the phrase which comes after Peter's denial, 'the Lord turned and looked at Peter' (22.60).

All these details are to be found in Luke's Gospel only, but whether he had extra information or was merely using an artist's licence we do not know. Other details peculiar to Luke serve to emphasize the serene faith of Jesus. It is true that there is a reference to his 'anguish of spirit' in Gethsemane (22.43), but Mark painted a darker picture in which 'horror and dismay' came over Jesus, who threw himself upon the ground in his grief and distress (14.34f.). Similarly, there is no cry of dereliction from the cross in Luke (contrast Mark 15.34); instead, Jesus utters words which were part of the evening prayer of a devout Jew, 'Father, into Thy hands I commit my spirit' (23.46), a prayer usually uttered in the faith that God would restore life in the morning. If that idea was in Luke's mind, the words here look forward to the resurrection.

The third quality emphasized by Luke in these chapters was the innocence of Jesus. He may have been anxious to refute contemporary accusations that the new Christian faith was politically subversive, although the evidence does not point clearly one way. However that may be, the charge before Pilate according to Luke was, 'We found this man subverting our nation, opposing the payment of taxes to Caesar, and claiming to be Messiah, a king' (23.2).

This is clearer, and perhaps historically more plausible, than the account in Mark, but even more significantly, Pilate in Luke was more reluctant to execute his prisoner; the phrase 'in his desire to release Jesus' (23.20) was added by Luke to Mark's version of what happened. Herod, too, is introduced as a further witness to the innocence of Jesus (23.15), and finally, the testimony of the centurion at the foot of the cross is changed in this Gospel to become, 'Beyond all doubt this man was innocent' (23.47).

One last feature of Luke's passion narrative should be noted here. In Mark the isolation of Jesus was complete. This is not so in Luke, who, whilst retaining Peter's denial (22.54–61) as an integral part of the story, suppressed Mark's reference to the desertion of the disciples (14.50) and Jesus' complaint that God, too, had forsaken him (15.34). Instead, Luke implied that Jesus' popular support did not evaporate entirely, and referred twice (23.48f., 55f.) to the women mentioned once in Mark, emphasizing in particular their Galilean origins. Why he did so is not clear. Perhaps he wished to show that the followers of Jesus were not guilty of wholesale apostasy; 'the way' began in Galilee, not in Jerusalem, although it could go no further than Jerusalem until there had happened 'what was bound to be fulfilled' (24.44).

Luke was strangely reticent about the significance of the death of Jesus. Ransom-language and references to sacrifice are almost entirely absent both in the Gospel and in Acts. The evangelist, for example, omitted Mark 10.45 with its phrase 'a ransom for many'. No satisfactory explanation has been given for this reticence, and yet in concluding this section we should note that Luke's silence in this matter is not total, as the narrative of the Last Supper (22.14–23) shows.

It is impossible to discuss here the immensely complicated problems about this meal. Was it a passover meal, or was it not? John and the first three Gospels differ. What exactly did Jesus say? (Compare Mark 14.22–24; Luke 22.19f.; I Cor. 11.24f.) What form and meaning did the Lord's Supper have in the early Christian communities? Apart from I Cor. 11.17–34, the evidence is tantalizingly fragmentary. And, finally, did Luke write 22.19f.? The manuscripts are not unanimous, as the footnotes in the *New English Bible* indicate.

But even if these questions cannot be answered with any certainty – and the debate goes on – and even if Luke attributed to Jesus only the words 'This is my body' (v. 19), they, together with the breaking and giving of the bread, were, in one sense, enough. The words were probably taken from Mark (14.22), but they indicate Luke's conviction, in spite of his usual avoidance of sacrificial language, that Jesus' death was an act of self-giving from which the life of the Christian community somehow stemmed.

### (v) 'He is risen'

To arrive at a proper understanding of the final chapters of Luke's Gospel some clearing of the ground is necessary, however disturbing this at first seems to be. First, there are contradictions about the resurrection appearances in the four Gospels which cannot be explained as the reports of different eye-witnesses. For example, Mark ended his Gospel with a prediction that the Risen Christ would appear to his disciples in Galilee (16.7); in Luke the first and only[14] appearance to the disciples occurred in Jerusalem (24.36–49). These differences between the evangelists are best explained in the light of what I said earlier (Chapters 1 and 2) about form criticism and redaction criticism; in other words, the influence of the early churches and the hand of each evangelist can be seen here also. This means that we are not dealing with straightforward accounts of what actually happened, and no doubt many readers today would readily agree that details such as the earthquake in Matthew (28.2) are legendary or symbolic.

What originally happened in terms of externally verifiable phenomena is impossible to determine, and people will quite legitimately differ about this. Christians affirm that God raised Jesus from the dead, and that means, for most of them at least, that Jesus lived – and lives – again. But it does not mean that he came back to life in the way we normally use that phrase. It means that he entered into a new kind of existence the precise nature of which cannot now be seen: 'Things beyond our seeing . . . prepared by God for those who love him' (I Cor. 2.9). Consequently, whilst nearly all Christians insist that faith in the Risen Christ is an indispensable part of Christian faith – indeed its bedrock – believing in a physical resurrection is not. (On this, see also Chapter 6, ii and iii.) The implications of this for understanding Luke 24.36–43 will be discussed below.

The first section of this chapter (24.1–11), describing the women's visit to the tomb, does not contain much, in its essence, of Luke himself. Here, it seems, he rewrote Mark's account with only one important change: the prediction of the angel that the disciples would see the risen Jesus in Galilee (Mark 16.7) becomes an invitation to them to remember what Jesus had said to them there (24.6f.). The main reason for this change was probably Luke's intention to keep all the action from now on in Jerusalem.

The superbly told story of the journey to Emmaus, found in this Gospel only (vv. 13–35), follows. A comparison of this narrative with the next story of Jesus' appearance to the eleven in Jerusalem helps to show why a healthy agnosticism about the precise nature of the resurrection is necessary. (Christian faith rests on a conviction *that* God raised Jesus, not on a theory about how he did so.) In the Emmaus story the disciples did not recognize Jesus, it seems, for a long time; in v. 37 the eleven disciples are at first petrified at the appearance of what they take to be Jesus' ghost. If we add to these details the evidence of the other Gospels, including the reference to the doubts of some disciples even, apparently, in the presence of the Risen Jesus (Matt. 28.17), it surely becomes clear that these narratives were intended not so much to convey information about the resurrection, as to proclaim it and indicate its meaning.

And so with the two appearances of the Risen Christ recounted by Luke, we shall be on the wrong track altogether if we regard them as factual accounts of what happened, and more nearly right if we ask what Luke meant by them.

In the first there is the familiar stress of this writer on the fulfilment of the Old Testament (vv. 25–27). This recurs in the next narrative. But perhaps the main impression which Luke's first readers would gain from this story would be the way in which past and present were interwoven. The climax comes in vv. 30 and 31: 'He took bread and said the blessing; he broke the bread and offered it to them. Then their eyes were opened, and they recognized him.' The crucial moment is recalled a little later on: 'They . . . told how he had been recognized by them in the breaking of the bread' (v. 35).

When was this? Once upon a time? Or whenever Christians in Rome or Corinth or Ephesus met to break bread together? According to Luke it was both then and now – in the past and in the present – for he told the story in a way which would remind his fellow Christians of their own communal meals or celebration of the Lord's Supper.

Our earlier discussion above about the nature of the resurrection raises the question of how we are to understand vv. 36–49, in which Jesus ate a piece of fish before the eyes of the disciples (vv. 42f.). This detail seems to contradict what Paul taught about the resurrection body ('flesh and blood can never possess the kingdom of God', I Cor. 15.50), unless we take the view that Jesus' resurrection appearances, being unique and unrepeatable, were the exception to the rule. That would not be the only difficulty, however, since eating food comes as near as anything can to offering proof of life. But the Gospels elsewhere give a portrait of a person who steadfastly refused to offer proof of anything. It is best, therefore, to acknowledge frankly that, whatever historical nucleus may lie behind this narrative, it cannot have happened like this, and that Luke developed the story for purposes of his own.

Nevertheless, when we try to discern Luke's purpose here, some valuable points emerge. In the church or churches for which Luke was writing, there may have been certain views about Jesus and his resurrection which Luke deemed untenable. Some perhaps regarded Jesus as an angel, or thought that he became an angel at his resurrection; others failed to connect the risen Christ with the figure on the cross. (The Corinthians probably made this last mistake, and a large part of I Corinthians is a corrective to their views. The church always makes this mistake if it chooses to celebrate Easter without taking seriously the implications of the cross.) In either case, Luke might have been saying to his contemporaries, 'The resurrection does not mean that Christians may live in a spiritual cloud-cuckooland of their own.' The unmistakable identity of the risen Jesus means that we may not forget, still less deny, the humanity of Jesus, with all that meant, and means, in terms of crucifixion and discipleship.

Verses 44 to 49 consist largely of words attributed to Jesus, but which are more likely to have been composed by Luke himself. What matters most is not who said them, but whether the evangelist correctly understood what Jesus and his resurrection really meant. Some themes which are given great prominence in Luke's second volume are mentioned here. First, the cross and resurrection represent the climax towards which the Old Testament was moving; Yahweh (the name of God in the Old Testament) had committed himself to bearing the burden and cost of creation, and although this comes almost in the 'stop press' column of the old scriptures, the conviction began to grow that even death was a sphere within, and not beyond, the power and purpose of God. Second, the more discerning spirits in Israel had seen for a long time that Yahweh was no mere tribal god, but God of all nations, and so now the resurrection was to be the impetus giving effect to this truth in a new faith and a new community. Finally, the disciples themselves would be equipped for the task of bearing witness (vv. 48f.).

With these great themes Luke had virtually ended his first volume. In it he had presented his faith that the way of the Messiah was the way by which the divine plan, inaugurated at creation, had to be fulfilled in order to bring about a major turning point in the history of the human race. But had the events of the decades which had elapsed between the time of Jesus and his own day justified the claims which the Christians were making for Jesus? Did they provide further evidence that things were going God's way? To these questions, amongst others, Luke addressed himself in his second volume.

# − 4 −

# Luke and the Early Church

(i) Beginnings

Because John's Gospel is sandwiched between Luke's two volumes, it is easy to forget that Luke wrote Acts as well as the Third Gospel, and that these two books were clearly intended to form one whole, as the first verse of Acts indicates. With his second volume, Luke was probably doing something quite new. There had been Gospels before, as he himself acknowledged, but this is the first history of the apostolic age of which we know.

At the end of the Gospel, Luke had reached a half-way stage in his epic. The scene has shifted from Bethlehem (and Nazareth) to Jerusalem. Now, as both the end of the Gospel (24.47) and the beginning of Acts (1.8) make clear, the holy city is to be the centre from which the new faith radiates outwards. Like other New Testament writers, such as Matthew and John, Luke believed that the time up to the crucifixion was in a special way the time of the Jews. The resurrection and ascension, however, are the sign that a much wider mission can now begin.

How, then, did Luke resume his work? The ascension of Jesus sets the scene for all that follows. Here, and here only in the New Testament, except perhaps Luke 24.51,[1] the ascension is an 'event' separate from the resurrection. Others referred to the resurrection only, or else wrote of the exaltation of Jesus (as did Paul in Phil. 2.9).

If we ask what this narrative signified for Luke, the answer is at least threefold. The cloud (v. 9) was a symbol of the divine presence, and therefore the ascension marked out Jesus as a very special man of God. Like Enoch, Moses and Elijah, his departure from the world could not be ordinary, because his closeness to God was more than ordinary. Secondly, for Luke the ascension meant the end of an era and the beginning of a new one. As in John's Gospel, the mission of the church

could begin only when Jesus had departed and the Spirit had been
given. Thirdly, by representing the disciples in the way he did, he
directed the attention of all would-be disciples from the wrong things
to the right thing. It was wrong, for instance, for the first disciples to
bother about when God would restore the kingdom to Israel (1.6f.).
The question and the answer given do not, of course, mean that poli-
tics are not the Christian's concern; the disciples are asking a religious,
not a political question. Luke portrayed them as wishing to know when
God would vindicate his people ('Lord, when will you make your
church strong and great again?'). That is, when will God intervene, or
act in a way which will brook no opposition and leave no room for
doubt? Such inquiries, however (vv. 7f.), are not legitimate concerns
for Christians, who will instead receive the resources to live in the world
as God's witnesses. It is equally mistaken to speculate about Christ's
return, or to watch for it (v. 11); it is enough to know that the last word
in history will lie with him.[2]

There was one further story to be recounted before the narrative of
volume two was well and truly launched. The original number of
apostles must be restored (1.15–26). The place of the election of
Matthias so early in Acts indicates how much Luke wished to emphasize
the apostolic nature of the church. They were *the* witnesses, and so
nothing could happen without them, and since Jesus originally chose
twelve, twelve there must be. Continuity was important. It was vital
that there should be people who had been with Jesus from the beginning, because they could now proclaim what they had seen and heard.
This suggests that their witness to his life mattered, as well as their
witness to his resurrection.

From Luke's standpoint it was not surprising that this should matter
so much. For him, belonging to the generation after the apostles, it was
essential that the church should continue their witness and obey their
teaching. In one sense, therefore, Luke held a doctrine of 'apostolic
succession'. The apostles were the 'sheet-anchors' at the Christian headquarters of Jerusalem (see 8.1 for example). They might have successors,
but there could be no more apostles after the first generation, as Paul
himself implied (I Cor. 9.1); the apostolic age was unique, and would
remain in the memory of the church as a golden age which the church
would draw inspiration from rather than emulate.

Before we leave the story of Matthias' election, a comment is necessary on Luke's distinctive way of describing things, and particularly of
describing divine guidance. This story is the only example in the New

Testament of Christians casting lots. It was a common enough practice in the world of the Old Testament (e.g. Num. 26.55), and in the Roman world, where it was sometimes used to check personal ambition. (That idea may have influenced Luke here.) Such a practice depended then on the belief that God or the gods would interfere, whereas now it rests on the assumption that there will be no human interference. Thus what Luke really wished to convey by this story was that the choice was really God's choice. Of course, even if the disciples had simply voted, that does not preclude a belief in divine guidance, but the story here reflects the view, expressed both in the Old Testament and the Dead Sea Scrolls, that God assigns to each person his 'lot' in life.

This way of understanding the election of Matthias is important for understanding many other stories in Luke's writings, particularly in Acts. It is being suggested here that Luke wrote up, or elaborated, something which actually happened in such a way as to bring out its significance, or else in order to get across a point to his readers. Sometimes he elaborated these bits of history by using, as here, ideas and images quite alien to modern thought, but this need not prevent us from appreciating his considerable artistry, and even more, the message he wished to communicate.

This approach applies also to the first 'miracle' recounted in Acts, the giving of the Holy Spirit (2.1–11). We are therefore dealing with a theological account of an event, the original nature of which it is now impossible to be sure about. The imagery of wind and fire is the clearest indication of this. When we ask, 'What was Luke trying to do here?', the answer seems to be that he wanted to explain at least three things. First, the Spirit of God – not just any spirit – was given to the disciples; without this gift nothing of what Luke goes on to narrate would have been possible. Secondly, the disciples received the gift of tongues, although it is not clear whether the tongues are foreign languages or glossolalia. Luke's account implies that one group (vv. 7f.) heard them as the former, and another group (v. 13) as the latter. Luke himself probably took the view that the disciples did indeed speak in foreign tongues. We cannot be sure precisely what happened, but we should note the view of one scholar:

If modern parallels (i.e. in modern Pentecostalism) tell us anything, then we must judge it to be quite probable that on the occasion itself (Pentecost) there were those who thought they recognized and understood words and phrases spoken by the disciples in their ecstasy.[3]

The third point Luke wished to convey here is made by the long list (vv. 9–11) of nationalities represented on this occasion. He was not thinking of Gentiles – this would make nonsense of later chapters, particularly Acts 15 – but of Jews from many parts who had taken up residence in Jerusalem (v. 5 says 'living' in Jerusalem, not 'staying' there). In this way he anticipated the 'catholic' nature of the emerging Christian church.

Whatever view we take of what actually happened and of some of the details in the narrative, the importance of the Holy Spirit in the Acts of the Apostles can hardly be over-estimated. Although at times Luke's veneration for the apostles – and for Paul, in particular – may seem to verge on hero worship, references to the Holy Spirit at key points in the narrative serve to show that the work of the early church was the work of God himself. The Spirit is responsible for major new departures in mission and evangelism (see e.g. 8.29; 10.33; 13.2f.), for the remarkable courage and confidence of the early disciples (e.g. 4.31), and for extraordinary acts of power (e.g. 13.9). The entire course of events which Luke narrated was in his view guided and determined by that same Spirit.

At the end of Acts 2, a picture of the life of the Christian community in Jerusalem is provided. Once again it is necessary to ask how far this description corresponds to the historical reality. Were things as marvellous as Luke implies?

It would be foolish to be dogmatic here, as indeed it would be with most of the other questions of history presented to us by the New Testament. It is unlikely that Luke invented the details of vv. 42–47 out of nothing. The Christians probably spent a lot of time in the Temple, because they expected the return of Jesus at any time, and surely the Temple, if anywhere, would be the scene of his appearing.[4] For this reason the 'Christian communism' practised by the disciples is not at all implausible. Why retain this world's goods if the End is so near? Luke's picture may reflect what actually happened, but, as usual, he worked up the reminiscences passed on to him, and gave his readers something slightly different: the church here is a mixture both of what it really was like, and also of what, in the writer's view, it ought to be like.

The last sentence, however, must be qualified at once. If we ask, 'What happened to the system of Christian communism practised in Jerusalem?', it would seem that it died out. We are given another description, including the generosity of Barnabas (4.34–37), but after that we hear no more of it. It is difficult not to conclude that the un-doubted poverty of the Jerusalem church later on (e.g. Acts 11.29; Gal. 2.10) was the consequence of this early enthusiastic experiment. It is perfectly possible, however, that this is a totally unwarranted, bourgeois interpretation. Certainly Luke did not intend his readers to see the sharing as a product of misguided enthusiasm, but more likely as the unique demonstration of the Spirit's power at the dawn of the church's 'golden age'. Perhaps because he saw this apostolic age as unique and unrepeatable, he could also regard their example as chal-lenging, inspiring and edifying, but not the norm for Christians of every age.

In fact, the New Testament contains various 'models' of Christian sharing. One of the most noteworthy in the writings of Paul is 'the collection', organized by the apostle in some Gentile churches to provide relief for the Christians in Jerusalem. Thus the New Testament as a whole suggests that the form which Christian sharing takes will vary according to circumstance. But whether the poor are in the same con-gregation, or in a different country, that sharing must occur.

(ii) Signs and wonders

Most modern readers of Acts will find it a bewildering mixture of 'natural' and 'supernatural' events. Angels intervene for good or ill; visions occur frequently; extraordinary miracles, both creative and destructive, take place. As in the Gospels, we have to allow for the contribution of the early churches and of Luke in the telling and re-telling of these stories, but we are still bound to ask whether events such as these are historical. As far as the healing miracles are concerned, it is likely that Luke did as he had done in his first volume and narrated the kind of thing that happened. The healing of the lame man (3.1–10) is one example, although the narrative is doubtless the product of Luke writing up a tradition or memory. But to deny that such healings occurred would be to be too sceptical by far. Indeed the modern church has begun to rediscover a healing ministry, even if undiscriminating attempts to emulate the New Testament in, for example, the practice of exorcism must be seriously questioned.

Nevertheless, whilst recognizing that extraordinary events surrounded the origin and growth of the Christian church, we still have to acknow-ledge that the miracles are one of the features of Acts most open to misunderstanding. To avoid this, we need to appreciate, as far as we can, the mind and purpose of Luke in telling the stories he did.

It was pointed out in Chapter 1 that Luke was not a historian in the modern sense of the word. He did not distinguish as sharply as we should between fact and fiction. This does not mean that he was distorting the facts; his concern, like that of other historians of his day, was to create out of his material an edifying narrative with a message for his readers. And so, once again, we are faced with an intriguing mixture of history, legend and commentary, the proportions of each varying according to the nature of the narrative.

To grasp clearly why Luke recounted miracles in this way it is useful to remember how full of Old Testament ideas his writings are. His view of miracles was that of some Old Testament writers: they are signs of God's presence, power and salvation. That is why some of the 'mighty works' in both the Gospel and Acts resemble those of Elijah and Elisha. Luke deliberately wrote them up like that. It is also important that we should let Luke's first volume shape our understanding of the second. Like those in the Gospel, the miracles in Acts are not only signs to doubters (Luke 7.22f.); they also mean liberation for the captive (e.g. Luke 13.16). Finally, in this respect, miracle and message are inseparable in both Gospel and Acts. Healings and sermons go together. The miracles confirm the preaching, and the preaching interprets the miracles; in Acts 3, for instance, Peter's sermon is a commentary on the healing of the lame man.

In Acts, then, miracles underline the rightness of the new faith. This is true also of what might be called the destructive miracles. The truth of the gospel, in Luke's view, can be seen by the fact that those who oppose it are swept aside. He clearly saw no problem about the way in which Ananias and Sapphira fall down dead at a word from Peter (5.1–11), Herod is struck down by the angel of the Lord (12.20–23) and Elymas is temporarily blinded by Saul (13.4–12). But these are difficult narratives for modern Christians, or at least for British Christians who are strangers to persecution and often opposition of any kind. We shall therefore consider each of these in turn.

The accounts of the deaths of Ananias and Sapphira can hardly be regarded as straightforwardly historical. Even if their deaths were brought about by overwhelming feelings of horror and guilt in an atmosphere overcharged with emotion, and even if their sin was or is regarded as 'the sin against the Holy Spirit' (Mark 3.29 and parallels Matt. 12.32; Luke 12.10), Peter's role in the story is frankly impossible to reconcile with the teaching of Jesus. The narrative therefore should be regarded as a legend with a message. Possibly Ananias and Sapphira had been the first Christians to die at a time when it was believed that no Christian would die before the Lord returned, and so their deaths came to be regarded as the penalty for particularly heinous sins which they must have committed.[5] However that may be, Luke used the story to point out the folly of being dishonest in the things which matter most of all, and of being half-hearted in Christian commitment.

The death of Herod is described also in the writings of Josephus, a Jewish historian who was a near contemporary of Luke's. He has no reference to an angel, but it is not surprising that the sudden and, for the Christians, timely death of Herod was interpreted by them as providential. That is surely what Luke was doing here.

As for the story of Elymas, Luke's attitude here and elsewhere (e.g. 19.11–20) seems to have been, 'Anything they can do, we Christians can do better'. Saul's battle with Elymas may have been meant to recall Aaron's contest with the magicians of Pharaoh (Ex. 7.8–13). His use of his apostolic power, like Peter's, inevitably gives us cause to wonder, but whether historical or not, the purpose of the story was to demonstrate that the power of the gospel was superior to that of contemporary magic (see also Chapter 5, iii).

This last miracle, like the deaths of Ananias and Sapphira, is one instance of what may be a conscious attempt by Luke to maintain a balance between Peter and Paul. Both heal a lame man (3.1–10; 14.8–18), and both bring a dead person back to life (9.36–43; 20.7–12). Both experience miraculous escapes from prison (12.1–17; 16.22–40), and both perform miracles of extraordinary power (4.15; 19.11f.). These parallels have led some scholars to conclude that Luke was anxious to show that the apostle to the Jews and the apostle to the Gentiles (Gal. 2.9) were equals. Not all the evidence, however, fits this theory, and it remains doubtful whether this was a paramount concern of Luke.

The place Luke gave to both creative and destructive miracles in Acts reflects his belief that miracles were a sign of God's presence with his church. These, and its rapid growth, were indications of the truth of its message. Perhaps the argument of the speech which he gave to Gamaliel was really his own:

... if this idea of theirs or its execution is of human origin, it will collapse; but if it is from God, you will never be able to put them down, and you risk finding yourselves at war with God' (vv. 38f.).

It is undoubtedly true that Luke wished to portray advances and successes; if there were mistakes and failures in this early period, we are not informed of them. There are references to controversy (6.1; 15.1ff., 37–39), but these are passing shadows across an account glowing with good teamwork and glorious success. In this matter Luke is sometimes compared unfavourably with Paul. Paul, it is said, has a theology of the cross, Luke a theology of glory. There is some truth in the contrast, as Luke's concentration on the church's successes shows. For example, he chose to give an extended account of the rescue of Peter from prison (12.1–17), preferring to do this rather than to give a long description of the martyrdoms of Stephen or James, perhaps because to have done so would have focussed attention on their heroism rather than on God's power. The view which a modern reader takes of Peter's escape will depend largely on his belief or disbelief in angels; but it is possible that what was originally a remarkable escape was attributed to God, whose 'intervention' was personified as an angel.

So Luke highlighted the spectacular and the extraordinary in his attempt to vindicate the Christian faith. In so doing he came close to implying that success is a criterion of truth. And yet history suggests that success is an ambiguous thing. The spread of both Communism and the Christian faith during the twentieth century has been remarkable in certain parts of the world. Similarly, a well-attended church may be a place where truth is proclaimed, but it may equally well be a place where prejudice is fed, and where people hear what they like to hear.

At this point we need to anticipate the theme of a later chapter (Ch. 7) and recognize that the New Testament offers several criteria for distinguishing truth from falsehood. The variety is instructive. Matthew suggests an ethical criterion: '. . . you will recognize them by their fruits' (7.20). The writer of the First Epistle of John puts forward a more theological one: 'This is how we may recognize the Spirit of God: every spirit which acknowledges that Jesus Christ has come in the flesh is from God, and every spirit which does not thus acknowledge Jesus is not from God' (4.2f.). Luke's criterion, too, must be taken seriously, and perhaps applied in reverse: a church which is *not* growing is not 'doing the truth' (a phrase from John 3.21). To that extent the Acts of the Apostles must be said to stand in judgment against us.

(iii) 'What God has done'

We should honestly admit that the opening chapters of Acts have given the modern church an inferiority complex. They have been used many times as the basis for unfavourable comparisons between the church then and the church now. Inevitably we are confronted by the questions, 'Was the church really like that?', and, 'Should the church always be like that?'

There will no doubt always be disagreement about the answer to the first question. Some will point to religious revivals of the past and of the present, and argue that similar things have continued to happen when Christians have had sufficient faith. They might argue further that 'with God all things are possible', and that it would be wrong to assume that success on the scale indicated by Luke was or is impossible.

However, without denying the force of these arguments, we must take other considerations into account. The superb artistry and dramatic power of Luke's narratives can easily lead us into thinking that from Pentecost to the conversion of Saul was a matter of weeks. It may have been, but it may also have been several years. Luke, in writing his second volume, compressed the history of perhaps twenty years into a mere fifteen chapters. The Council of Jerusalem, described in Acts 15, is generally thought to have taken place around AD 50. So there are good reasons for thinking that Luke chose to give his readers a series of 'de Mille' spectaculars, a succession of powerful pictures, like an edited version of a football or cricket match on television, in which only the highlights are shown. But was it all as dramatic or as breathtaking as that?

There is a further reason for thinking that Luke was concerned more with making an impression on his readers than in presenting a strictly factual account. According to Acts (2.41), three thousand people were converted on the day of Pentecost, and many more on subsequent occasions (5.14). But even if as many as three thousand could be within earshot of someone speaking in the open air, it is unlikely that the Christian community in Jerusalem was as large as this. And so, if we accept the number as historical, we should accept also the suggestion that many of the converts were Jews from abroad who returned home after the Feast of Pentecost.[6]

In the opening chapters of Acts, therefore, we are not dealing with a factual day-by-day account of the Christian church, but with a series of impressionistic vignettes, based on historical events for the most part, but written up by Luke in a way intended to edify Christian churches of his own day, and perhaps to instruct the inquiring pagan. (This is less certain; some features of Luke's work suggest it was intended for a wider public, but on the whole, like the rest of the New Testament, it

seems to have been written for a church, or for a group of churches.) It
is tempting to call Acts a piece of propaganda, and so, in a sense, it is.
But since propaganda tends to be an emotive, disparaging word, Luke's
second volume is best called an 'evangelical history'.

A look at the sermons in Acts will provide further light on the author's
approach to his work. I have suggested elsewhere (*Was Jesus Divine?*,
pp. 64–6) that they should be thought of as Luke's own commentary on
the proceedings, rather like the voice-over on a television documentary.
The sermons may have been built around genuine reminiscences of
what was actually said on each occasion, but the finished products are
Luke's, and they serve as a theological commentary on the events which
he narrates.

The sermons of Paul will be discussed in the next chapter, and that
of Stephen in the next section, but the sermons and speeches of Peter
occur as follows: 1. the sermon at Pentecost (2.14–36); 2. the sermon in
the Temple after the healing of the lame man (3.12–26); 3. the speech
before 'the rulers, elders and scribes' in Jerusalem (4.8–12); 4. the
speech before the Sanhedrin (5.29–32); 5. the sermon in the house of
Cornelius (10.34–43); 6. Peter's defence in Jerusalem of his sermon to
Gentiles (11.4–17).

If we compare these passages, several themes emerge quite frequently.
Appeal is made to the Old Testament: prophecies there 'prove' that
God's Messiah was to suffer and rise again (e.g. 4.11; 2.25–28), and that
God's Spirit would be given in a new and powerful way (2.17–21). The
witness of the apostles is another frequent feature (2.32; 3.15; 5.32;
10.41), and most sermons end with an appeal for repentance and faith,
the outcome of which will be forgiveness and the gift of the Spirit (e.g.
2.38). Two of these passages also contain references to the life of Jesus
(2.22 and 10.38), one a reference to his return (3.20f.), and one to the
last judgment (10.42).

Although they are always directed to specific situations, the sermons
have a certain uniformity about them. They are presumably outlines or
summaries of what Luke deemed to be 'model' sermons for Jews, or,
as in Acts 10, for Gentiles sympathetic to, or informed about, Judaism.
For this reason the fulfilment of the Old Testament figures very pro-
minently; the quotations given here were doubtless the product of much
intensive study of the Jewish scriptures by Christians in the first years
and decades after the resurrection. Since the audiences in these early
chapters are usually Jewish, one might have expected more lengthy
explanations of the crucifixion, which, as Paul saw so clearly, was a

'stumbling-block' to Jews (I Cor. 1.23). Instead, much greater prominence is given to the resurrection. This, for Luke, was God's great vindication of Jesus, which confirmed the God-centredness of all that preceded it, including the cross.

The question arises of whether this preaching should be regarded as a model for all subsequent preachers. The answer is both 'yes' and 'no'. The particularity of each sermon forbids a literal imitation of Luke. In spite of the similarities we have noted, the content and terminology vary to suit the occasion. For example, the use of the Old Testament title 'servant' (e.g. 3.13) as a title for Jesus, if not a reminiscence of what Peter actually said, probably reflects Luke's attempt to make the sermon sound as Jewish as possible. In other words, the audience determines the choice of words. With that in mind, we may surely regard the sermons as 'models' for preaching in that their contents, and their emphasis upon scripture, Christ and the Spirit, can be summed up as 'what God has done'.

Finally, the speeches of Peter hint at what is to come. They make clear that the new faith is not a new-fangled religion, but the fulfilment of the old; Jews and Christians are talking about the same God (e.g. 3.13). The leaders of this new movement are not self-appointed preachers; it would be easier not to preach, but they must obey God rather than men (4.19; 5.29), a familiar argument to any educated Greek or Roman. Both these assertions lead to a third: the ancient scriptures and the contemporary pressure of God point in the direction of the Gentiles; for 'God has no favourites' (10.34), and he had promised Abraham that 'in your offspring all the families on earth shall find blessing' (3.25).

## (iv) Jew and Gentile

The opening chapters of Acts portray a new movement which goes from strength to strength. Nothing can stop its growth, and persecution only contributes to its advance (8.1, 4). However, it was far from being a new religion, for to many outward observers at least, it remained a party or a sect within Judaism. But how long would it remain so? How far could, or should, the gospel spread?

The largest single controversy in the first few decades after the crucifixion and resurrection of Jesus was whether the gospel was for Gentiles as well as for Jews, and this question dominates the pages of Acts more than any other theme. It was the note on which the Gospel ended

(24.47); it is hinted at in the opening verses of Acts (1.8), and it is the central issue at the end (28.17–27). The prominence of this theme is hardly surprising in view of the enormous revolution in thought and attitude implied by it. All the first Christians were Jews, and remained Jews when they became Christians, just as many Methodists in the eighteenth century continued to be Anglicans. This was true of the Christians who spoke Aramaic, and those who spoke Greek, although the latter, being more liberal, became the prime targets of persecution and probably produced the leaders who were responsible for extending the scope of the Christian mission (6.5; 8.1–5; 11.19–24).

According to Acts (6.1–6), the leader of the Greek-speaking Christians in Jerusalem was Stephen. The speech given to him in Acts 7 is by far the longest in Acts, much of it being devoted to the special place of the Jews as God's chosen people. Its main theme, however, is 'like fathers, like sons' (v. 51). Just as Paul agonized over the question of how the chosen race could possibly have rejected the Messiah (Rom. 9–11), so Stephen's speech seems designed to show that such a rejection was only the last in a long series of rebellions. This meant that, so far from casting doubt on the Christian faith, the Old Testament confirmed it negatively as well as positively, for the response of the Jews was both predicted and predictable. Luke, therefore, probably intended this speech to signal the end of an era. 'The time of the Jews' was passing, and the 'time of the Gentiles' was about to begin. The quotation from Isaiah at the very end of Acts, 'this people has grown gross at heart; their ears are dull and their eyes are closed' (28.27), implies that this transitional process was now complete.

As often in the New Testament, we are faced with a document which is both intensely Jewish and, in a sense, anti-Jewish. One devout Jew after another is presented in the narratives of Luke-Acts – Simeon, Anna, Joseph of Arimathea, Barnabas, and most important of all, Paul himself – but Jewish opposition provides a constant back-cloth throughout. How are we to resolve this paradox?

In Old Testament times there grew up a belief in a 'faithful remnant'. However faithless the majority of Israel might be, there would always be some who remained faithful to God. Paul himself used this idea (Rom. 11.1ff.). It is one which may easily become the guiding principle of exclusive, intolerant sects, but at its best the concept of a 'remnant' bears witness to the belief that God's work in the world is often done through small, rather than large, numbers of people, and that growth can emerge even out of old, apparently lifeless institutions. The first

Christians came to believe that this was what was happening in their day. As the remnant, they proved to be the nucleus of a new people of God.

Luke gives the impression that the process by which this growth came about was a natural, orderly progression. Here he had the benefit of hindsight, and the conviction that God's guiding hand directed the whole process. The reality was probably much more piecemeal and untidy. The story of Philip and the Ethiopian eunuch (8.26–40) may preserve a memory that Philip had been a great missionary pioneer, and Antioch (11.20) was undoubtedly a church renowned for its 'outreach'. But pride of place in this first ecclesiastical revolution was reserved, according to Luke, for Peter, whose visit to the Gentile Cornelius is described at length (10.1–48). The space Luke devoted to it indicated its crucial importance. As if to make sure, he told the story twice, for in Acts 11 he has Peter retell it – ostensibly for the church leaders in Jerusalem, but in reality for the reader. The climax of the long story and, for Luke, the heart of the matter comes in Peter's rhetorical question at the end: '. . . how could I possibly stand in God's way?' (11.17).

The preceding paragraph prepared the way for this. Peter was merely the instrument of a divine plan which surprised him at every turn. The vision which rebuked his unjustified scruples about consorting with Gentiles (10.9–16, 28f.; 11.5–10) and the gift of the Spirit before he had had time to start or finish (see 10.44; 11.15) his sermon are two of the features by which Luke made his point: this was the work of God.

In the chapters which follow, Luke omitted, or did not know of, a good deal of conflict and controversy. Most probably he decided to deal with it, and get it out of the way, in one single chapter (ch. 15). This describes an amicable compromise, the so-called Apostolic Decree,[7] between the conservatives in the church led by James, and those who were missionaries to the Gentiles. There is, however, a major historical problem here. Scholars have debated for a long time whether the conference described by Luke in this chapter was the event referred to by Paul in Gal. 2.9. Since Paul in his letters nowhere refers to the Apostolic Decree or gives any indication that he even knew of it, it must be doubted whether he attended such a meeting, or, if he did, whether he agreed with its decision. The problem cannot be resolved conclusively. But if there was a kind of summit-meeting at this point in the history of the young church, it did not end the controversy about Gentile converts, as the letters of Paul make clear. Nevertheless, Luke's overall view is correct. A decisive breakthrough was achieved, however piecemeal and gradual it may have been. Chapter 15 is thus a turning point in the story: after this Peter is heard of no more, and Paul occupies the centre of the stage.

# – 5 –

# Paul

In the last chapter we looked at some of the features of the church as Luke presents them in the early chapters of Acts. Now we turn to the man who increasingly dominates the narrative – Paul.

Most people who have any knowledge of Paul usually have a picture of him drawn – whether they know it or not – from two sources: the Acts of the Apostles and Paul's own letters. It is not often realized that there are differences, and even discrepancies, between these sources, and these discrepancies must be examined first in order to appreciate the particular aims and achievements of Luke.

## (i) One Paul or two?

It may be said at once that we should not be surprised to find a difference between what a man says about himself and what a 'fan' writes of him a generation or so later. This is especially so when a person has been very controversial or divisive. For example, biographies or appreciations of men such as Marx, Freud or de Gaulle will not only differ from each other (depending on whether the writers were 'pro-' or 'anti-'); they will also differ from their subjects' own evaluation of themselves. In the same way we must be prepared for quite different perspectives and viewpoints when we compare Paul's own writings with Luke's portrait of him.

In the first place, Paul addressed himself to controversies of the moment: should the Christians of Corinth eat meat which had been offered to idols (I Cor. 8)? Should the Christians of Galatia be circumcised (Gal. 1.6ff. etc.)? What are the Christians at Thessaly to believe about those of their number who had died (I Thess. 4.13ff.)? And so on.

These controversies also included his own status as an apostle, which was hotly disputed (see, e.g. I Cor. 9.1), and his version of the gospel, which was fiercely contested, or misunderstood, or deliberately misrepresented (Gal. 1.7–9; Rom. 6.1; 3.8). We can still hear echoes of some of these controversies in the narratives of Acts. For example, Luke knew that Paul had not been exactly popular with many Jewish Christians, as the words he gives to James and the elders show (Acts 21.20–22). But by Luke's day the dust had settled and Paul's own position as a Christian hero was assured, even though Luke for the most part restricted the title 'apostle' to the Twelve only (see Chapter 7).

Yet in spite of the difference of perspective and interest which is clearly there in the writings of the two men, there are still a number of discrepancies which indicate that Luke's information about Paul was not entirely accurate, or else that he wished to present him in a particular way. We noted some of them in Chapter 1, but more might be added to that list. Luke implies that Paul was a good speaker; the Corinthians, who presumably had heard him, said that he was not (II Cor. 10.10). He describes him as a Roman citizen (e.g. Acts 16.37), whereas the apostle himself makes no mention of it. Most important of all, he presents Paul as a Christian Pharisee, faithful to the Jewish Law (e.g. Acts 23.6). Paul himself wrote to the Christians at Philippi (Phil. 3.5–7) as if his Pharisaism were a thing of the past.

These details do not comprise all the differences between the Epistles and Acts by any means. And clearly some are more of a problem than others. One might argue, for example, that Paul never had occasion to mention his Roman citizenship in his own letters, but the difference over his Pharisaism and his attitude to the Jewish Law is much more complicated. Luke portrays Paul as a moderate figure who goes out of his way to satisfy Jewish scruples. For instance, he accepts the advice of James (21.23ff.), which may be regarded as an example of what Paul himself says: 'To Jews I became like a Jew' (I Cor. 9.20). However, it is very difficult to reconcile the circumcision of Timothy (Acts 16.1–4) with the stand which Paul says he took on the question of Titus' circumcision (Gal. 2.3–5). Most notorious of all, would the 'real' Paul have agreed to the final 'communiqué' issued by the Jerusalem summit in Acts 15? That final communiqué, as we noted in the previous chapter, finds no mention at all in Paul's letters, and many scholars question whether he knew anything about it.

These last differences obviously call into question the accuracy of Luke. It is often said that Luke was an accurate, conscientious historian, and there is undoubtedly evidence to support this view. But, as our discussion in Chapter 1 also showed, it is equally impossible to deny that Luke got some things wrong. In the examples we have mentioned, we have to say either that Paul was not consistent or laid himself open to grave misunderstandings, or that Luke recorded a tradition which was not entirely correct. As for the 'Apostolic Decree', it may be that Luke projected back into the previous generation a compromise between Jewish and Gentile Christians which was in force in at least part of the church in his own day.

In this matter it is important that we try to arrive at a balanced picture of Luke's work. It would be wrong to think that Luke simply gave free rein to his imagination, regardless of facts, or that he was consciously writing what we would call edifying fiction. On the other hand, he clearly was writing up his material, sometimes quite freely, in a way that suggests he preferred to contradict himself rather than weary his readers with repetitions. It is also important not to exaggerate the differences between Acts and the Epistles, but at the same time not to ignore or minimize them either. The real Paul, to judge from his letters to Corinth and Galatia, was a more stormy, controversial character than Luke implies. And so in one sense we have two Pauls in the New Testament, not one, and in the next chapter we shall consider the significance and value of this fact.

It is a mistake to imagine that the two Pauls must somehow be harmonized – that is, fitted together in a way that removes or explains the differences. It is no more desirable or possible to do this than it is to harmonize the Jesus of Mark and the Jesus of Luke. The New Testament gives us different impressions of its two most important figures, and we should attempt to learn what we can from each writer, allowing his impression to speak on its own terms.

## (ii) Paul's conversion

By far the best-known description of Paul's conversion is the one to be found in Acts 9.1–19. There are, however, two more accounts in Acts 22.3–21 and Acts 26.12–19, and a careful comparison of all three passages shows that they offer a striking example of the point made in the previous section: Luke preferred to contradict himself rather than repeat himself word for word. So, for instance, according to 9.7 those travelling with Paul (Saul in Hebrew) to Damascus heard the voice but saw no one, but in the second account (22.9) they 'saw the light', but did not hear the voice. More striking still is the account in 22.17ff. of a vision not recounted elsewhere. The differences must not be exaggerated, since many of the details remain the same. But, again, Luke used an artist's licence to tell the story in a slightly different way each time. He also adapted the story to suit the situation; the vision in the Temple (22.17ff.), for example, is recounted in the setting of the Temple.

A glance at Paul's own letters strengthens the view that we should be careful of saying that Luke's account states exactly what happened. Paul's much briefer descriptions of his 'conversion' experience have no references to the Damascus road, to a blinding light, or to Ananias. Nothing he says contradicts Luke's accounts; but his silence about details such as these means that we are left wondering to what extent Luke elaborated the traditions he received. In fact, it is impossible to say where Luke got his information from, and his version should probably be seen as a compound of history and artistry. But that, of course, would be no less legitimate than a dramatic presentation in a church of another famous conversion, such as that of Luther or Wesley.

The fact that Luke recounted this event three times is a measure of its importance for him. There was no more epoch-making occurrence in the history of the church than the admission of the Gentiles, and although we cannot assume that Paul was the only pioneer in this matter, he may well have been the Gentile mission's leading 'intellectual', who developed the theology implicit in the enterprise.

So two things at least are clear from Luke's three varying accounts of Paul's conversion: they are not purely factual in content, and, secondly, Luke believed that this event was supremely important. But now we must go on to consider what Luke or Paul for that matter, does *not* say. Neither, contrary to what is a very widely held view, says that the apostle's conversion was the result of a prolonged heart-searching or of a struggle against his conscience. One reason why it has been thought to be so is the Greek proverb included in the text of the Authorized Version at Acts 9.5: 'It is hard for thee to kick against the pricks.' But these words are found in only one manuscript at this point, and so were probably not written by Luke here. The only certain place where they occur is 26.14, but even there the 'pricks' do not mean 'pricks of conscience'; the proverb means 'Opposition to me is senseless and impossible' (Haenchen, p. 685, quoting Bauernfeind).

The other main source for the view that Paul's conversion was the outcome of a long inner struggle is Romans 7.7–25, where Paul used the word 'I'. However, a growing number of scholars do not think that

Paul was describing himself here as he was before he became a Christian: for example, 'the good which I want to do, I fail to do' (v. 18). It is more likely that the 'I' here is 'everyman', and Paul wrote in this way to lend greater vividness and directness to his words. But it is not autobiography. Indeed, his description of himself elsewhere (Phil. 3.6) suggests that he was a successful Jew, not a failed one. If Luke is correct in saying, as he does at 7.58 and 22.20, that Saul witnessed the death of Stephen, this would strengthen the view that his persecution of the church became increasingly doubt-ridden. Such a view is possible if we can assume, first, that Luke is historically accurate here and, secondly, that Stephen's death had this effect on him.

There are some interesting implications here for Christian faith. First, the hymn 'Just as I am', with lines such as,

> Fightings and fears within, without,
> O Lamb of God, I come!

has often been thought of as a classical expression of a normal conversion experience. But, without denying the validity or significance of this hymn, it must be said that we cannot assume that Paul's conversion was of this type. And if we do, we may well be simply projecting on to him our own religious experience.

A second result of the approach outlined above is that we may see more clearly that Paul did not 'change' his religion. For this reason 'conversion' can be a misleading term. He had been a Jew and he remained a Jew, albeit a very different one. He continued to worship the same God as before, although in a very different spirit. He remained utterly committed to and convinced of the heritage of the Old Testament. But now he believed that the crucified Messiah was its fulfilment. Luke's accounts, in fact, bring out this religious continuity, admittedly at the price of obscuring the radical change which occurred in Paul's attitude to the Law. Luke, it seems, wished to emphasize that the new faith was the natural child of Judaism and the fulfilment of the Old Testament, and although it is only one side of the picture, it has important implications for our attitude to and use of the Old Testament today.

What, then, happened to Paul? Both Luke and Paul are agreed that through this crucial experience, whatever its precise nature, he received a commission to preach the gospel to the Gentiles. And so his conversion should be seen like the other experiences of the Risen Lord, as primarily a call to service involving a 'repentance' of the most profound kind. That is, many of the principles and scruples dearest to Paul's heart must be sacrificed. Above all, the fundamental division of mankind into Jew and Gentile had to go; it still remained, of course, but it was no longer fundamental. Although Paul continued to believe that the Jews had had a head start in the matter of salvation (e.g. Rom. 3.1f.) – that was simply a historical fact – the whole world was God's and all people were his.

### (iii) Paul's travels and preaching

People who have attended Sunday schools have usually endured a few sessions on the missionary journeys of St Paul, and might be forgiven for thinking that to know where Paul went, by what route and in what order, was one of those things necessary for salvation. As with so much else in Acts, we can no longer be sure that Luke presented things with complete accuracy. It is possible to match up Acts and Epistles here and there – for example, there is a rough, though not exact correspondence between I Thess. 3.1 and Acts 17.14–16 – but for the most part the information yielded by Paul's own writings is fragmentary, and that given by Acts not always reconcilable even with that.

The reference to Gallio, the proconsul of Achaea (18.11), and to Festus, the procurator of Judaea (24.27), make it possible to date Paul's travels approximately. We know from an inscription discovered in Greece that Gallio was proconsul at Corinth from AD 51–52, and from the writings of contemporary historians such as Josephus, that Festus, and his predecessor Felix, probably held office in Judaea in the middle or late fifties. So it seems that most of Paul's travels took place in the decade from AD 50 to 60.

It would be foolish, however, to become preoccupied with the minutiae of Luke's geography and chronology. To do so would be to fail to see the wood for the trees. Luke gave an impressionistic account, and we must allow his picture to speak for itself. It is an impressive enough picture, with many of the great urban centres of the eastern Mediterranean – Athens, Corinth, Ephesus and Antioch – being depicted, sometimes with rich local colouring. (This is especially true of Athens and Ephesus.)

It was in the cities of the Roman Empire where, according to Luke, Paul's preaching was done. In the previous chapter it was suggested that the early sermons in Acts are the author's summaries of the kind of thing the apostles said or what the author thought appropriate to each occasion. This applies also to the three sermons attributed to Paul

(13.16ff.; 17.22ff.; 20.18ff.), each of which was addressed to a quite different group. The first, at Antioch in Pisidia, was preached to Jews; the second, at Athens, to Gentiles; and the third, at Miletus, to Christians. We shall look briefly at each of these.

The theme at Antioch, as one might expect in a sermon preached to Jews, is the fulfilment of the Old Testament. After a brief resumé of Old Testament history from the Exodus to David, Paul proceeds to argue that Jesus is the fulfilment of the promise made to the fathers (i.e. Abraham, Isaac and Jacob), and that his resurrection was foretold in the Psalms. Most modern readers of Acts are likely to be unenthusiastic about such arguments. The early Christians' use of the Old Testament often seems strange, highly selective and sometimes bizarre. But this at least can be said. It is possible and desirable to see Jesus as the fulfilment of the Old Testament in a way broader and deeper than that which sees him as the fulfilment of a few well-known yet isolated passages such as Isaiah 53 ('but he was pierced for our transgressions . . .', v. 5a) which, strangely enough, features relatively little in the New Testament. Sometimes, in fact, Luke refers to Jesus and the fulfilment of scripture without referring to specific texts, and whilst we clearly cannot speak of Jesus as the fulfilment of the whole of the Old Testament, we may say that the Old Testament represents a movement (with blind alleys and diversions on the way) towards him. Luke did not fill in all the details, but clues are provided by the way in which Paul, for example, described Jesus as the wisdom of God (e.g. I Cor. 1.24), and this suggests that Jesus may be regarded as the 'fulfilment' of the book of Job, even though 'Messiah' is never mentioned there. The point is that Job was a 'wisdom' book and, as Paul Tillich suggested,[1] it is doubtful whether the men of the New Testament could have lived with the cross without that Old Testament background.

The second sermon at Athens is more famous. These verses from Acts may be seen today on a plaque at the spot where Paul is thought to have preached. (Or was he on trial?)[2] Yet scholars are still divided over whether Paul would ever have said these words. It is true that there are a few verses in Romans which describe God's revelation through nature and through the moral law (Rom. 1.19f.; 2.14–16), but there is nothing in Paul's writings to correspond to the quotation from the pagan poet Aratus ('We are his offspring', v. 28), and the complete absence of any reference to the crucifixion is hard to reconcile with what Paul said about his preaching in I Corinthians (1.23). It will not suffice to say that Paul failed here because he did not preach 'the true

gospel'. Luke, as we saw in the last chapter, did not record failures or
mistakes in Acts, and the sermons are undoubtedly intended to be
thought of as apostolic examples of good and not bad preaching. This
sermon, then, must be seen as Luke's understanding of how Paul would
have preached the gospel to Gentiles with no conventional (i.e. Jewish)
background whatsoever.

Paul starts from where his listeners are, by referring to a sanctuary
of theirs and by citing, not scripture, but a writer whose authority they
would regard more highly than the Old Testament. In fact, of the nine
and a half verses which make up the sermon, seven and a half are
devoted to showing that there is a good deal of common ground between the Christian and the so-called pagan. They can both agree about
a creator God who does not live in man-made temples (vv. 24f.), who
is the God of all people (v. 26), and who is nearer to man than man
realizes (vv. 27f.).

The distinctively Christian section is confined to the last two verses
(vv. 30f.). It can hardly be argued that this is a watered-down or trun-
cated version of the gospel, for the resurrection is mentioned, and Luke
regarded that, not unreasonably, as the keystone of the new faith.

Whatever we may think of the merits or defects of this sermon, it is
clearly intended to be an essay in Christian apologetic. It is a standing
reminder that Christian preaching may have many forms, taking seriously the situation of its hearers, and adapting both its arguments and
language accordingly. The fast-changing, diverse society we now live in
requires of modern preachers that we at least aspire to the versatility of
Luke.

The position of the sermon at Miletus in the narrative of Acts is
significant. This is the last occasion in Acts when Paul is amongst
friends,[3] able to speak his mind and to offer the church his parting
legacy. The speech reads rather like a last will and testament, and no
doubt Luke intended that. After this the way for Paul will grow darker,
as the speech itself indicates (vv. 22f.), and for the church as a whole
things will never be quite the same again (vv. 29f.). It is as if Luke was
looking back on the time of the apostles as a 'golden age', when advance,
spectacular miracles and success were the order of the day. Thereafter,
as these words imply, Christians will live in a period of consolidation
and retrenchment.

That is why Luke's own hand can be seen more clearly here than in
many other places in Acts. It seems that in writing his speech he had
two questions in mind:

1. How would Paul have summarized his life's work?
2. What would Paul have to say to us in our day (i.e. Luke's day) if he could have foreseen our situation and our problems?

Verses 18–27 contain Luke's answer to the first question, vv. 29–32 his answer to the second, and vv. 33–35 provide a fitting coda to the whole of Paul's apostolic life and work. Even if the answers are Luke's, it must be said that there are one or two striking echoes of the Epistles,[4] and some themes which are quite fundamental to Paul's own thought.

The first theme is Paul's own faithfulness to the commission he received from Christ. That commission was to preach the grace of God in Christ, and in this matter Paul placed all his cards on the table; he held nothing back (vv. 20, 27). It is possible that Luke wished to emphasize in these verses the courage of the apostle: in spite of opposition he did not trim his gospel (as the Galatians accused him of doing). The Gentiles to whom Paul preached received no watered-down presentation of the gospel, nor were they given a kind of second-class gospel, with the full version reserved for a spiritual élite. (The situations in both Corinth and Galatia show how easily such accusations might arise.)

In facing their own problems, the leaders of Luke's own church are reminded of two things: they are to shepherd the flock and to remember Paul. Both points are important and related. Leadership in the New Testament is always crucially important, and can be properly done only in the spirit and after the example of the apostles. Not surprisingly, this leads on to the essence of apostolic authority and ministry (vv. 33–35). By emphasizing that this essence is self-denying service, Luke was at one with the historical Paul himself, and of course with the saying 'I am among you as one who serves' (Luke 22.27).

One further feature of Paul's life and work as Luke portrayed them is the miraculous or supernatural element. From the start, Paul's ministry is accompanied by extraordinary happenings which have traditionally been called miracles, and directed by divine providence. His first missionary journey opens with a dramatic miracle, involving the public defeat of a distinguished magician (13.1–12). It is possible that Luke's concern here may have been to show that Christian 'magic' was greatly superior to pagan magic (see the previous chapter). But even if this is so, Luke's placing of this miracle at the very outset of Paul's travels is dramatic enough: it encapsulates the conflict in which Paul will be engaged throughout his life, and Luke wished his readers to be in no doubt that, 'Those who are on our side are more than those on theirs' (II Kings 6.16).

If he described a somewhat 'negative' miracle in ch. 13, a more positive one follows in the next chapter (14.8ff.). Once again it is shown that Christian faith is to do with wholeness and with the mending of broken lives. The lame man is healed at Lystra, and the reaction of the crowds brings out in sharper relief the humility of the apostles. Their miracles are not an ego trip, making them celebrities overnight. They mediate a power not their own.

Accounts of other miracles follow in later chapters. A 'possessed' slave girl is healed at Philippi (16.16–18). A young man called Eutychus who had fallen from an upstairs window in the Christians' meeting place at Troas was restored to life (20.7–12).[5] The father of the leading citizen on Malta is cured of fever and dysentery (28.7–10). Most remarkable of all, we are told that Paul's healing power could be transmitted to the sick via handkerchieves and the like (19.11f.).

It is certain that extraordinary happenings, called 'signs and wonders' in the New Testament, accompanied the ministry of Paul. He himself alluded to them (Rom. 15.19; II Cor. 12.12), but he did not state what they were, and they clearly did not silence his critics and opponents. But are Luke's stories about Paul fact or fiction, history or legend? No certain conclusions can be drawn, but if Luke wrote up what actually happened, he did so in ways calculated to achieve the maximum dramatic effect. We may, however, wonder whether the miracles mentioned in 19.11f. really happened, and if we do regard them as historical, we must concede that little room is left here for faith, and the danger of magic and superstitition is very real.

One final point may be made here about the way in which Luke chose to portray the apostle Paul. From start to finish he is led by divine guidance and protected by divine providence; the Spirit inaugurated his work (13.2), and thereafter directed its course (16.8–10), and divine encouragement came in the most unexpected places (18.10). This feature becomes more prominent in the last section of Acts, to which we now turn.

(iv) The last journey

Acts 21–28 comprises almost exactly one quarter of the book, and yet, with the possible exception of ch. 27, this is probably the least-known part of Luke's work. It may be useful first of all, therefore, to summarize the content.

In the previous section we saw how Luke presented the farewell speech at Miletus almost as Paul's last will and testament. But he used it also to show that the storm was gathering and the shadows lengthening (v. 23). The dramatic tension heightens in the following chapter, 21, as the final stages of the apostle's journey to Jerusalem are punctuated by prophecies of suffering and imprisonment (vv. 4, 10f.). Paul nevertheless goes on, and, on his arrival, agrees with James and the other Christian elders upon a plan[6] designed to pacify not only the non-Christian Jews, but also those Christians who were still almost fanatically Jewish in their adherence to the Law. Here the tensions of the early Christian churches are unmistakable. James and his colleagues may well have been liberally disposed towards Paul, but they had to cope with arch-conservatives within the Jerusalem church who felt that Paul had been too radical in his mission to Gentiles, and they also no doubt wished to retain some standing with those fellow-Jews whom they still hoped would become Christians.

Had the plan worked (v. 27), as it almost did, Paul presumably would have been religiously acceptable in Jerusalem and could have continued with his plan to take the gospel to the far west (Rom. 15.25–33). It failed because Jews from Asia instigated a riot in the Temple precincts from which Paul was rescued only by Roman intervention (21.27–40).

From this point Luke began his account of Paul's imprisonment and trial. It used to be thought that he was writing notes for Paul's defence counsel in Rome, but it is more likely that he was weaving together past history and contemporary concerns in a way relevant to the problems of his readers. The speeches, in particular, of Paul are intended to show that the Christian mission to the Gentiles was God's will and that the new faith was the natural heir – indeed the true expression – of Judaism. As we saw in the previous chapter, Luke may have done this partly for political reasons.

These are the concerns which lie behind the dramatic but rather implausible scenes which follow Paul's arrest (21.27–22.30).[7] Historical or not, some of the points would be clear enough to Luke's readers. For example, the crowd's throwing dust in the air (22.23) was a way of dissociating themselves from blasphemy,[8] whilst the tribune's strange remark to Paul about 'the Egyptian' (21.38) made clear that Christianity was not a movement of wild fanatics engaging in misguided ventures.

Luke's concerns reappear in the even stranger scene which follows (22.30–23.10), when Paul appears before the Sanhedrin and the high priest. His abuse of the high priest, followed by his apology (23.1–5),

may again seem most implausible, but it served to illustrate Luke's conviction that the Jews, not the Christians, were the real transgressors of
the Law. As for Paul's ploy in setting Sadducee against Pharisee in a
theological cat-and-dog fight (vv. 6–9), it can only be said that the real
Paul would never have uttered the words of v. 6, particularly 'I am a
Pharisee'. But Luke made his point. Even though Jews may quarrel
amongst themselves, Christians and real Jews have no grounds for
quarrelling.

More drama follows when Paul's nephew unearths a Jewish plot to
kill the apostle and promptly informs the Roman tribune, who sends
Paul under armed guard to face the procurator Felix at Caesarea
(23.12ff.). Paul's appearance before Felix is then recounted, a scene
which may owe more to Luke's imagination than anything else, but, as
always, Luke's message for his contemporaries comes through: Christians, so far from being trouble-makers, are law-abiding members of the
Way, united with true Jews in their hope of resurrection (vv. 10–21).

Felix first adjourned Paul's case (24.22f.), and later kept him in
custody because the Jews possibly bribed him to do so (vv. 24–27). His
successor, Festus, is also depicted as a procurator bent on humouring
the Jews, and his proposal that the trial be transferred to Jerusalem is
the immediate cause of Paul's dramatic appeal to Caesar (25.11), which
ensured a trial in Rome. Luke, however, was anxious not to portray
Roman officials in too bad a light. In the next section Festus is a well-
meaning official who is at a loss to know what to do with his controversial
prisoner. King Agrippa, too, comes before us as something of 'an
authority on Jewish problems' (Haenchen, p. 674), and so the outcome
of Paul's audience with them both is particularly significant:

> 'This man,' they said, 'is doing nothing that deserves death or im-
> prisonment.' Agrippa said to Festus, 'The fellow could have been
> discharged, if he had not appealed to the Emperor' (26.31f.).

The audience before Agrippa is presented in a way which brings to
a climax Luke's own presentation of the claims of the Christian faith.
After that it only remained for him to describe an eventful sea-voyage
(ch. 27), Paul's brief stay on Malta (28.1–10), his arrival in Rome
(28.11–15), and his discussions with the leading members of the Jewish
community there (vv. 17–27). Finally, the book closes with the claim
that Paul continued to preach and teach for two years whilst under
'house arrest' (vv. 28–31).

What did Luke intend to communicate to his readers by these chapters? It is not surprising that they are less well-known than earlier sections of Acts. There are no inspiring set-piece sermons, few miracles, and, apart from Paul himself, no inspiring examples for Luke's church to emulate. Instead, the story of Paul's arrest, trial and journey to Rome is spread over no less than eight chapters.

It is here, above all, that Luke's short-term aims are most apparent. He was writing for his contemporaries, perhaps not even for the next generation, still less ourselves. His preoccupation was one which we have seen to be a major concern of his all along: to make clear to his Christian contemporaries, and perhaps to contemporary unbelievers as well, how the church came to be where it now was. The mission to the Gentiles did not mean that here was a dubious new religion; it was the fulfilment of the old. The Christians were not trouble-makers, still less political agitators, but were obeying the God who had spoken through the Jewish religion in times past.

These are the concerns which lie behind the protestations of Paul's innocence and of his Jewishness. Some scholars argue that Luke was disloyal to Paul here: for example, would the apostle himself have made no mention of the cross in a speech such as that before Felix (24.10ff.), which meant also that none of the radical statements about the Jewish Law, made in Paul's epistles (e.g. Gal. 3.13, 'the curse of the Law'), find a place in Acts? We have to answer 'No' to such questions; the real Paul would surely not have expressed himself thus. Although Luke's reticence about the cross remains a mystery, there is some justification for his approach. Then, as now, having faith that God vindicated beyond death an executed man is the cornerstone of Christian believing.

Another characteristic prominent in these chapters is Luke's concern with VIPs, especially Romans. The Roman tribune Lysias, Felix, Festus, Agrippa and Bernice come and go. Luke's portraits of them might be interpreted as a wish to catch prestigious converts, and that may indeed have been a motive, but his approach must also be seen as thoroughly catholic. The very style of his prologue – the fact that it was written at all – had given notice of his intent: Christian faith was no longer an obscure sect in a provincial backwater, but a faith with catholic claims.

So there remains to the very end in Acts a strong note of success and triumph. For this reason Luke has not been without critics who have questioned whether he had really taken to heart the message of the cross. But though at times he seems to sing the praises of Paul rather than of God (e.g. perhaps 28.1–10), there are sufficient reminders of divine guidance to show to the reader that this new phenomenon called 'The

Way' was 'from God', and so no-one would finally be able to stop it (Gamaliel's argument in 5.38f.). If Luke makes it sound all too easy, it is worth remembering that he and his contemporaries lived under the threat, if not the reality, of persecution, and so the cross can hardly have been devoid of all significance. It may be that our difficulties, in the Western world at least, with some features of Luke's thought are a reflection upon ourselves and our shortcomings as well as upon the limitations of his theology.

But there is a final point to be made here about the man who has dominated the whole of the second half of Acts. For reasons of his own, Luke chose not to mention 'the collection', a project which Paul mentioned at some length in his epistles (Rom. 15.25–32; I Cor. 16.1–4; II Cor. 8; 9). This was intended to raise monetary or material assistance for the poverty-stricken mother church at Jerusalem, but Paul regarded it not only as famine relief and a gesture of goodwill, but also as an expression of the unity of Jewish and Gentile believers, and perhaps also as a sign of the end. But he was apprehensive about its reception in Jerusalem (Rom. 15.31). Did the church in Jerusalem accept it? Or did they feel, faced with growing nationalism among their co-patriots and with zealots in their own church, that they could not? The pages of Acts are silent. It seems unlikely that Luke did not know about the collection; indeed, Acts 20.4 could possibly be a list of the people who represented the churches involved. And so it is possible that Paul's visit to Jerusalem was a much more personally shattering experience than Luke allows us to see. All his cherished hopes and plans may have come to nothing. He certainly led no mission to Spain, and an 'ecumene' or union of Christian Jews and Gentiles must have seemed a pipe-dream. As often in the Bible, future growth and development lay on the far side of apparent failure and defeat. Paul's reception in Jerusalem, as well as his later fate in Rome, amply justified Luke's deliberate echoes in these chapters of an earlier journey to Jerusalem which he had already described in his first volume. And yet, as in the time of Jesus, so now in the days of the church, Luke's narration of the onward march of events reflected his conviction that things were going God's way.

# – 6 –

# The Nature and Purpose of Luke's Writings

The last four chapters have been devoted to a survey of each of Luke's two volumes in turn. In this chapter we shall be looking at Luke-Acts as a whole. The separation of the Gospel from Acts in the New Testament makes it more difficult to appreciate their unity, but the reference to Theophilus at the beginning of each book makes it clear that we are dealing with the work of one writer. So, too, do the many similarities in style and language. As for the author's own view of his task, there are enough literary and theological connections between the two volumes to suggest that he himself envisaged his work as a whole. For example, if Luke wrote the phrase 'and was carried up into heaven'[1] at the end of the Gospel (24.51), we have two references, not one, to the ascension in his work. The repetition in greater detail at the beginning of Acts (1.1–11) provides a theological 'clamp' by which Luke's work is held together.

There are more pervasive themes linking Luke's Gospel and Acts, and some of these will be considered in the next section in an attempt to outline the particular theological convictions he sought to express. But first it is important to appreciate the gap, both in time and culture, between Luke and ourselves.

As we saw in Chapter 1, scholars vary in their conclusions about the nature of Luke's work. Some stress his theological achievement, others his reliability as a historian. Many recognize in Luke-Acts a combination of both theology and history, and that is the view taken here. It is necessary, however, to guard against attributing to Luke a modern approach to either theology or the writing of history. We must not saddle him with modern theological concepts and problems, even though we may hope that his work will sometimes throw light on our situation.

Nor must we gauge by modern standards his achievements as a historian.

There is another danger to guard against here. When Luke, or any other biblical writer, is studied, it is necessary to remember that he was writing for his contemporaries and not for future generations. Modern readers are 'eavesdropping' on a first-century conversation which took place between the author and his first readers. Of course, such listening in will be little more than an academic exercise if we are not open to the possibility that the word of God may reach us through these ancient writings. But it is vitally important to try to hear first what Luke was saying to his original readers; otherwise there remains the danger of reading into his work modern ideas, beliefs and prejudices.

It must be said, however, that it is not easy to perceive the situation for which Luke was writing. It was suggested in Chapter 1 that he wrote towards the end of the first century in one of the large cities of the Roman Empire, perhaps in Rome itself, and that Luke's readers, or hearers, in the first instance, would have been his local church or a group of local churches. But can any more be said about them?

It is reasonable to suppose that much of the material included in Luke-Acts was thought by its author to be particularly relevant for the situation for which he was writing. If that is so, several conclusions can be drawn about Luke's readers. It is likely that they came from both the rich and poor sections of society, from the upper classes as well as the lower classes. Recent sociological studies of the New Testament documents have modified an older view that Christianity was primarily the religion of slaves. Slaves there were, and at Corinth the majority, though not the whole, of the congregation, consisted of people from the humbler sections of society (I Cor. 1.26). But the prominence of teaching about the use of wealth in Luke-Acts suggests that there were Christians of various social positions in the communities for which Luke wrote. This view is strengthened by the frequent references to hospitality. Jesus himself is a guest on several occasions (e.g. Luke 14.1) and in Acts Peter is the guest of Simon the Tanner (Acts 9.43; 10.6), and Paul and his companions stay at the house of Lydia (16.14f.). Other examples could be given from Luke-Acts and from other early Christian writings of the prevalence and importance attached to the practice of hospitality. The prominence accorded to this by Luke, however historically accurate some of the instances may be, surely reflects the social situation of many of his fellow Christians living, as they almost certainly did, in a commercial and political centre of the Roman Empire.

The problems faced by Luke's churches cannot be easily discerned. The writer does not seem to preach at his readers; for all his re-writing, he often allows the tradition to speak for itself. We can be fairly certain, however, that persecution, if not actual, was always possible (Acts 14.22). We may also surmise that there were teachers challenging the legacy of the apostles (Acts 20.29). The main challenge probably came from those advocating the rejection of the Old Testament and the church's Jewish roots. Marcion in the next century was the most powerful advocate of this view, but the battle had probably already begun in Luke's day. Paul in his time had battled to ensure that the new faith should not be confined to Jews, and that Gentiles who became Christians should not be obliged to become Jews as well. The conflict of the next period was about whether the Christian churches should sever themselves entirely from their Jewish past.

Lastly, we should not forget Luke's view of both the past and the future. In the period after the fall of Jerusalem in AD 70 most, if not all, of the apostles had died and the mother church of Jerusalem no longer existed as a unifying centre. Therefore someone was needed to present to Christians an interpretation of both their origins and their apostolic past. Secondly, Luke, unlike Paul and perhaps Mark, did not expect the end of the world in the immediate future. This, too, is part of the setting against which any assessment of Luke as a theologian must be made.

## (i) Luke as a theologian

In this matter it is not easy to get Luke right. We have rejected the over-simple view that Luke was a kind of Greek or Palestinian Dr Cameron who wrote 'the most beautiful book in the world'. Many of his stories are indeed incomparable, but it is all too easy to wrap Luke's writings in a warm, sentimental haze, and so miss their full force.

On the other hand, as we saw in Chapter 1, some question-marks have to be set against the approaches of many German scholars of the last half-century. Luke does not seem to have been a sophisticated theologian, whose every word was pregnant with hidden meaning, and the work of Conzelmann, amongst others, must be regarded as being over-subtle at times in its approach to Luke-Acts. It is equally unsatisfactory to treat Luke-Acts as a theological make-weight in the New Testament canon, its presence in scripture being tolerated rather than valued. This may be to caricature the views of scholars such as Rudolf

Bultmann and Ernst Käsemann, but their unfavourable comparisons of
Luke with Paul or John do not always do justice to Luke.

The title 'theologian of salvation history' has frequently been be-
stowed upon Luke. It can be misleading for at least two reasons. First,
it suggests that Luke set himself a theological task rather like a modern
theologian, and, secondly, the term 'salvation history', which has been
extremely common in New Testament scholarship, conjures up a picture of a kind of holy channel running through 'ordinary' history, with
no real connection between the two. In spite of the misleading nature
of these terms, it will be useful to consider the qualities of Luke's work
which evoked them.

Luke-Acts forms an impressive tapestry, a biblical epic whose sub-
title might well be 'From Jerusalem to Rome' or 'God's Purpose in
History'. Its scope is truly comprehensive, ranging from the birth of
John the Baptist with its echoes of the first book of the Old Testament,
to the very Greek-sounding events at Athens (Acts 17.16–34), and the
splendid tale of the shipwreck in Acts 27, surely a literary 'set-piece'.[2]
But although the variety and scope are immense, the underlying theme
is quite simple: in Paul's words, 'From first to last this has been the
work of God' (II Cor. 5.18). This message is conveyed in several un-
obtrusive, yet unmistakable, ways. We noted in Chapter 2 how the
many Old Testament echoes, particularly in the opening chapters of
the Gospel, invited the reader to see that in Jesus God was continuing
and fulfilling what he had been doing throughout Israel's history. Again
and again Luke emphasized the continuity between the Old and the
New Covenants, a message vitally relevant to his contemporaries not
only for political reasons, but also because, as we have seen, there were
emerging, or there were soon to emerge, people in the churches who
wished to reject the Jewish heritage into which Christians had entered.[3]

A second way in which Luke indicated that God was at work in all
the events he was narrating was by means of a short but very significant
Greek word *dei*. This word, meaning literally 'it is necessary that . . .',
comes to mean in the writings of Luke, 'It is part of God's plan that . . .'
It is a word which is found more in Luke-Acts than in any other New
Testament book; in fact Luke-Acts accounts for almost half its total
occurrences in the New Testament. It occurs regularly throughout the
Gospel: 'I must (*dei*) give the good news of the Kingdom of God . . .'
(4.43); 'The Son of Man has to (*dei*) undergo great sufferings . . .'
(9.22). *Dei* occurs even more frequently in Acts. The apostles 'had to'
obey God rather than man (5.29), and Paul 'had to' see Rome and stand

before Caesar (19.21; 27.24), because, as Luke implied by using this word, it was God's will that he should. Thus Luke indicated to his readers that the whole march of events was under the direction of God.

So far these aspects of Luke's 'theology' were shared by other New Testament writers in varying degrees. Others, notably Matthew, emphasized the fulfilment of the Old Testament, and many used the word *dei*, although not as frequently as Luke. The distinctiveness of Luke, not surprisingly, emerges more clearly in his second volume, where the many parallels between Jesus and the apostles enlarge still further his presentation of 'salvation history'. The apostles were those who were witnesses 'from the beginning' in Galilee (Chapter 2, ii). In particular, as the sermons in Acts make clear time and again, they were the witnesses of the resurrection. Thus they constituted the vital link between the time of Jesus and the time of the church, and became the 'pillars' of the church, a title used by Paul in referring to the three leading apostles (Gal. 2.9).

We may note here that there are two views in the New Testament about what is 'the church's one foundation'. According to Paul (I Cor. 3.11), there can be no foundation other than Jesus Christ, whereas the Letter to the Ephesians (2.20) describes the apostles and prophets as the foundation.[4] If, however, we understand the essential characteristic of an apostle to be that of faithfulness to the spirit and teaching of Jesus, there is no real contradiction. Luke's way of looking at the matter is that of the writer to the Ephesians, but the parallels between his first and second volumes help to convey the apostles' faithfulness to and dependence upon Jesus himself.

The rabbis had a saying, 'The one who is sent is as the one who sent him', and the word 'apostle' reflects this, since it was probably derived from the Hebrew *shaliah*, meaning 'emissary'. This idea is never far from the surface in Acts. The healing of the lame man (Acts 3.1–10) is the first dramatic enactment of the words found in John's Gospel: 'In truth, in very truth I tell you, he who has faith in me will do what I am doing; and he will do greater things still' (14.12). Peter's raising of Tabitha (Acts 9.36–43) recalls, and may be meant to recall, the raising of Jairus' daughter.[5] The power communicated even by Peter's shadow (5.15) and by Paul's body (19.11f.) is, Luke implies, like the power which emanated from Jesus (6.19). Finally, Paul's progress to Rome is strangely reminiscent of Jesus' journey to Jerusalem (see especially 19.21; 20.22f. and 21.14). In these and other ways we are reminded that the Acts of the Apostles are really the acts of the emissaries of Jesus.

The parallels, however, extend further. Luke believed that Jesus had empowered his disciples to speak with the same power and authority as he had done. On several occasions Jesus' opponents were left speechless (e.g. Luke 20.7, 8, 26); similarly, the apostles left the authorities with nothing to say (Acts 4.14; 6.10). People reacted to Jesus' words by either repenting and believing, or by anger and even fury; responses to the apostles' preaching were no different (compare Luke 15.1 with Acts 5.14, and Luke 4.28 with Acts 7.54).

The story of Stephen contains the greatest number of parallels with the ministry of Jesus. He is introduced to the reader in language reminiscent of Jesus: 'a man full of faith and of the Holy Spirit' (Acts 6.5; compare Luke 4.1); 'Stephen, who was full of grace and power, began to work miracles and signs among the people' (Acts 6.8; compare Luke 24.19). Like Moses, and perhaps like Jesus, Stephen's face was radiant (Ex. 34.29, 35; Luke 9.29; Acts 6.15). Like Jesus, he was led out of the city to meet his death (7.58), and his final prayers are the most notable parallel of all: 'Lord Jesus, receive my spirit' (7.59; compare Luke 23.46), and 'Lord, do not hold this sin against them' (7.60; compare Luke 23.34).

It is difficult to escape the conclusion that behind all these parallels is an understanding of the apostles not unlike that of the Fourth Gospel: 'As the Father sent me, so I send you' (John 20.21). In the light of all this, it is easy to see why Luke has been called 'the theologian of salvation history'. He offered his readers a panoramic view of the history within which God had initiated his plan for the world, decisively demonstrated and furthered it in Jesus, and was even now continuing it in the life of the church.

There is another theme running throughout Luke-Acts which must be mentioned here. From Luke's vantage-point, as we have seen, the most significant development had been the way in which the 'people of God' had broadened to include Gentiles as well as Jews, and so, not surprisingly, he emphasized in many places and in many ways that the gospel is for all. The *Nunc Dimittis* – 'a light to lighten the Gentiles' – is one of the earliest indications of this (2.29–32), although the shepherds of the nativity narrative, earlier in the same chapter, are the first of many 'outsiders' who feature in the Gospel. Luke's genealogy in 3.23–38 traces Jesus' ancestry back to Adam, the father of the human race (contrast Matthew's genealogy, which begins with Abraham). In the following chapter, where Luke announces Jesus' programme by means of the sermon at Nazareth, the references to Elijah's and Elisha's ministries to Gentiles (vv. 25–27) make clear which way the wind is blowing.

Examples can be multiplied. But here is one of the most important features of God's plan according to Luke. 'Outsiders', such as women, Gentiles, Samaritans and tax-collectors, are welcome. An apt commentary on the social background of the Gospel is provided by a rabbi's prayer (although it probably comes from a slightly later period):

> Blessed art Thou, O Lord our God, King of the Universe, who hast not made me a Gentile. Blessed art Thou . . . who hast not made me a slave. Blessed art Thou . . . who hast not made me a woman.[6]

In Luke's first volume the universality of the gospel is potential, rather than actual; it is foreshadowed, rather than realized. It is only in Acts, in fulfilment of the promise that the disciples would be witnesses 'to the ends of the earth' (Acts 1.8), that the Gentile mission was properly begun. Luke was well aware what a momentous step this was, since as we saw in Chapter 5, the commissioning of Paul was recounted no less than three times, and the conversion of Cornelius – in one sense the first Gentile believer – twice, whilst the watershed of the book (ch. 15) describes a summit meeting at Jerusalem on this very subject.

It is clear to us that the future lay with Paul and with those who thought like him. Perhaps it was even then clear to Luke, since he focussed his attention almost exclusively on Paul in the second half of Acts. Even the church at Jerusalem fades out of sight. What mattered in Luke's view was that Paul should reach Rome, and when that had been narrated, Luke was content to lay down his pen.

There has been a lot of discussion about why Luke ended the narrative where he did. Quite apart from the size of a papyrus roll – it is noteworthy that the Gospel and Acts are almost exactly the same length – the answer does not seem to be, as used to be thought, that Acts was written whilst Paul was awaiting trial in Rome, and therefore Luke could not include a reference to his death. In ending where he did, Luke had amply demonstrated the universality of the new faith. The centre of gravity had shifted from Jerusalem to Rome; the extended quotation from Isaiah (Acts 28.26f.), in particular, sets the seal on this. But in order to show that it was an unfinished story, the book ends not so much with a full stop as with a series of dots:

> He stayed there two full years at his own expense, with a welcome for all who came to him, proclaiming the kingdom of God and teach-

ing the facts about the Lord Jesus Christ quite openly and without
hindrance . . . (28.30f.).

In this way Christian faith burst out of the bounds of Judaism. A
Jewish sect became a catholic church. The world had been taken by
storm and would never be the same again.

It follows from this that Luke wanted to put Christianity on the map.
His introduction, following as it does the literary conventions of the
day, suggests as much. So, too, do the references to the census (2.1) and
the various officials, Jewish and Roman (3.1), at the time when John
began his ministry. Even someone as worldly as Augustus Caesar, and a
character as dissolute as Tiberius Caesar, are mentioned in this Gospel.
It may be that Luke had a 'political' purpose here. He was anxious to
claim for Christianity the status of *religio licita* – a permitted religion –
from the Romans, a status which had been accorded to the Jewish faith.
That could be one reason why he emphasized the continuity of Judaism
and Christianity. But, apart from this, he also wished to show that the
origins of Christian faith were not a 'hole-and-corner' business (Acts
26.26). It was a faith for all reasonable people – it was not unthinkable
that even King Agrippa should become a Christian (26.28f.). The same
theme emerges in the story of Paul's visit to Athens, for, whatever the
history behind this scene, Luke was staking a claim here for the new
faith in the intellectual centre of the world. Paul himself can hold his
own with the philosophers of the day. He can even manage a quotation
from a Greek poet (17.28).

The panorama presented by Luke-Acts is one of the most impressive
qualities of Luke's work. On the one hand there emerges the continuity
of God's dealings with the human race, reaching back into the Old
Testament as far as creation itself, and reaching forward into the in-
definite future into which the Spirit leads the church. On the other hand,
the all-embracing nature of God's plan emerges equally clearly. The
good news is offered to all, to the religious and the irreligious, the
principled and the unprincipled, in a cosmic perspective which calls to
mind Paul's claim for Jesus in the Second Letter to the Corinthians:
'God was in Christ reconciling the world to himself' (II Cor. 5.19).
This brings us to the heart of Luke's message, which is Jesus himself.

The language Luke uses to describe the work of Jesus and his rela-
tion to God is in many ways very different from that of other New
Testament writers such as Paul and John. It is often more 'low-key'.
Jesus is described as 'a man singled out by God' (Acts 2.22), and 'a man

of his (i.e. God's) choosing' (Acts 17.31). He is called a prophet (Luke 24.19) and even refers to himself as a prophet (Luke 13.33). This is not the whole picture; Jesus is also called 'Lord', 'Son of God' and 'Saviour', as elsewhere in the New Testament, but on the whole Luke has far less of the exalted language which the other writers use.

It is impossible to do justice here to all the titles of Jesus in Luke-Acts, or to the ways in which Luke expounded his achievement and significance. We shall confine ourselves to noting one of the most important and pervasive themes. It can best be summarized by the verse of Paul quoted earlier in this section: 'From first to last this has been the work of God' (II Cor. 5.18). This is a theme frequently introduced by Luke into the conclusions of the gospel miracle stories. Scholars have shown that the evangelists reworded their material most freely when writing the introductions and conclusions of such stories. (This was not so, however, when the conclusion consisted of words of Jesus which, on the whole, they altered less freely.) When we examine Luke's conclusions, it is noticeable how frequently the word 'God' appears. Those who have been healed are often said to 'glorify God' (e.g. Luke 18.43); they do not, as a rule, thank Jesus. The story of the ten lepers (17.11–19) is an exception, although even there thanking Jesus seems to be equated with praising God (vv. 16, 18). The most striking examples of this motif, however, occur in the raising of the widow's son at Nain (7.11–17), and the healing of the epileptic boy (9.37a–43). The conclusions to these stories include the following phrases: 'Deep awe fell upon them all, and they praised God . . . they said . . . "God has shown his care for his people" ' (7.16), and 'they were all struck with awe at the majesty of God' (9.43). These and other such verses do not mean that Luke thought of Jesus quite simply as God in human form. To attribute to him later ideas about the divinity of Jesus and the incarnation is rather like crediting Isaac Newton with a knowledge of the theory of relativity. But Luke was undoubtedly saying that God was at work in Jesus. The sermons in Acts reinforce this by their allusions to what God did through him: 'Jesus of Nazareth, a man . . . made known to you through miracles, portents, and signs, which God worked among you through him' (Acts 2.22), 'He went about doing good, and healing all who were oppressed by the devil, for God was with him' (Acts 10.38). So, although we are a long way in Luke-Acts from the later language of the Trinity, Luke emphasized time and again that the person and work of Jesus were God-centred from start to finish.

The claim that it was God himself at work lies, as we saw in Chapter

4, behind the many references to the Holy Spirit in the Acts of the Apostles. Just as the work of Jesus was the work of God, so the activity of the Holy Spirit is the activity of God. Again, the language is far from trinitarian, but the echoes of the Old Testament and the parallels between Jesus and the apostles reflect Luke's belief in the consistency and unity of God's operations in the world. These assertions, of course, are not historical in the normal sense of that word. That is to say, the historian cannot prove or disprove that God acts in his world. It is not part of his task, not least because evidence for such claims cannot be assessed in the way that historical data usually are. In spite of the risk of wrapping everything in a haze of mystery and paradox, it must be said that they are a matter of faith. But it would be difficult to deny that such claims are at the very heart of Luke's work.

## (ii) Luke as a historian

The subject of Luke's reliability as a historian was briefly touched upon in Chapter 1, where I argued that the value of his writings cannot be assessed solely by how accurate he was in every detail. Luke was an ancient writer, not a modern one, and a good deal of evidence has been presented in the last four chapters to show that he did not aim at the kind of historical accuracy which a modern historian would be expected to attain. He modified the narrative of Mark, and not all his alterations can be accounted for by the theory that he had access to extra information. Similarly, we have noted some of the discrepancies between Acts and the Epistles of Paul, not all of which can be explained by the different aims and circumstances of the two writers. Yet when all this has been said, we are still a long way from implying that Luke-Acts is little more than edifying fiction or even that its author was highly tendentious in his approach. The question is not *whether* Luke adapted his sources, but rather how dependent he was upon them for his material, and *how much* he adapted them.

On this subject widely diverging views exist amongst scholars. Howard Marshall, a British scholar, has emphasized Luke's faithfulness to his sources,[7] whilst in Germany recently Martin Hengel has made an assessment of the historical value of Acts which is much less sceptical than those of many post-war German scholars.[8] On the other hand, scholars such as John Drury, writing on the Gospel, and Ernst Haenchen, writing on Acts, believe that Luke composed freely and extensively. The variety of opinion is not surprising in view of how little we know about the sources Luke used. His sources for Acts cannot be identified, and although archaeology has verified a few details of his account, we can do little more than balance his narratives against the information to be gleaned from other New Testament documents, chiefly the letters of Paul. In the case of the Gospel, if Luke used only Mark and Matthew as his sources, the extent of his own composition was very considerable. On this view Matthew's Gospel must have been revised and edited so thoroughly that hardly a trace of Matthew's original arrangement remains in Luke's work. (This was not, however, true of Mark, whose order Luke largely retained.) But if the traditional view is correct that Luke drew upon two other sources (usually referred to as Q and L) besides Mark for his Gospel, then it can be argued that the extent of his own editorial work was more limited. It is unlikely that the debate will ever be finally settled, and for this reason any assessment of Luke as a historian must be a tentative one.

Nevertheless, there are indications that Luke allowed the traditions he knew to impose, to some extent, restrictions upon his editorial activity. It seems that he did not feel free to do whatever he liked with the material. There are features in his writings which he might have been tempted to leave out because of the possibility of misunderstanding and even offence. He wanted to emphasize that Jesus had not been politically subversive (Luke 23.14), nor were his followers (e.g. Acts 24.5, 12f.). This may have been why he toned down the harshness of a saying of Jesus he knew of, 'I came not to bring peace but a sword' (Matt. 10.34). In Luke's Gospel this saying becomes, 'Do you suppose I came to establish peace upon earth? No indeed, I have come to bring division' (12.51). But he did not omit it altogether, nor did he leave out the story of the cleansing of the Temple (19.45f.), or the admittedly obscure saying about the two swords (22.35–38). For similar reasons he might have chosen to omit the words, 'If anyone comes to me and does not hate his father and mother, wife and children, brothers and sisters, even his own life, he cannot be a disciple of mine' (14.26). Roman society set great store by the quality of *pietas*, a word which signified being to one's father and mother all that a good son ought to be. Yet Luke retained the saying in what was probably its original severity. Matthew, as we noted in Chapter 3, preferred to write, 'No man is worthy of me who *cares more* for father or mother than for me . . .' (10.37).

Other examples can be given of Luke's faithfulness to the tradition. The Jewish origins of Jesus are emphasized, rather than played down, and the phrase 'the Son of Man', which probably dropped out of use very early on in Christian preaching to the Gentiles, is still extensively used. Lastly, Luke's veneration for the apostles did not prevent him from including the story of Peter's denial, or the quarrel of Barnabas and Paul (Luke 22.54–61; Acts 16.37–39).

Of course, some of this material may have been so familiar in Luke's day that the evangelist could hardly have left it out of his writing even if he had wanted to. It is also difficult to be sure about Luke's own preferences, and possible causes of controversy or offence amongst his contemporaries. But the details given above, and the concern of the author, alluded to in Chapter 1, for the correct background 'colouring', may be signs that he conscientiously carried out the aims of his preface, however conventional its wording: '. . . to give you authentic knowledge about the matters of which you have been informed' (Luke 1.4).

### (iii) The importance of Luke-Acts

For many years there has been a school of thought amongst New Testament scholars that historical knowledge about Jesus was virtually impossible to obtain, and, secondly, that it was not important for Christian faith. Rudolf Bultmann was the most influential exponent of this view, arguing that, although the life and teaching of Jesus were the necessary prelude to the crucifixion, God's word to man through the cross of Christ was the heart of the Christian message. A verse in Paul's Second Letter to Corinth seemed to him to underline the unimportance of knowing Jesus historically: '. . . even if we had known Christ in the flesh, we do so now no longer' (5.16). (The translation of the *New English Bible* is rather different, and the Greek in fact, may be interpreted in various ways.)

Bultmann was reacting against the scholarship of an earlier generation, and believed that faith should not be dependent on history. For him it was unthinkable that Christian faith should be vulnerable to historical investigation. How could the word of God possibly be undermined by the evidence or argument of a historian? The question is a complex one, and the debate goes on. Most scholars now think that Bultmann, for all his undoubted greatness as a scholar and interpreter of the New Testament, was too negative in his conclusions about what we may know of Jesus. Many would also argue that the life and teaching of Jesus are more important for Christian faith than he allowed.

We are concerned here with the significance and value of Luke-Acts, and it is noteworthy that Bultmann based his interpretation of the New

Testament almost entirely on Paul and the Gospel of John. It is well known that references to the life and teaching of Jesus in Paul's writings are few,[9] and in John's Gospel, although scholars now think that it contains more historical information about Jesus than an earlier generation had thought, the historical figure of Jesus has been largely transformed into the heavenly Christ of Christian faith and devotion. Not surprisingly, Bultmann valued the writings of Luke less highly than the work of Paul and John.

The Christian faith, however, is not simply a message out of the blue. It is also a historical phenomenon; its historical origins are important, and so, too, are the continuities of history. And if the crucifixion should be understood as the inevitable outcome of what Jesus stood for, said and did, as it surely should, then all that preceded it cannot be dismissed simply as 'prolegomena'. The achievement of Luke was to take seriously the historical task implied here, but to write his history in the theological tradition of the Old Testament. The outcome of his work was an epic which, for all its rich detail, was thoroughly Christ-centred and therefore God-centred. For this reason Luke-Acts must be regarded as an important part of the diversity to be found within the New Testament. In the next chapter we shall examine this diversity by comparing some themes in Luke's writings with the ways in which other New Testament writers have handled them.

# − 7 −

## Unity without Uniformity:
## Luke and Other New Testament Writers

In the previous chapter we looked at Luke's writings as a whole, considering both their theological and their historical content. It is now time to set his work in a wider context and consider its similarities to and differences from other New Testament writings. This is a necessary task, because recent scholarship has made it increasingly clear that the New Testament does not have a single uniform theology. There is an underlying unity, but in order to perceive that, its rich diversity must first be appreciated. In this chapter, therefore, we shall survey the variety on a number of themes within Luke-Acts itself, and then go on to examine Luke's theology in relation to that of other New Testament writers.

### (i) The age of the Spirit

Paul, Luke and John, in their different ways, teach that Christians live in the age of the Spirit. No New Testament writer denies this, although none is as concerned as these three with that particular theme. Within that age Christians must live 'apostolically', that is to say, they must work out the implications of their discipleship and their commission from Christ in faithfulness to him before the end comes. We are concerned in this section with the variety on these subjects both within Luke-Acts itself, and also amongst other New Testament writers in comparison with Luke.

It would be difficult to exaggerate the importance attributed by Luke to the Holy Spirit. From the start of his epic to the end, he made clear that the work of God in the world was effected only by his Spirit. The Spirit fills Elizabeth, Zacharias and Simeon (1.41, 67; 2.25), heightening their spiritual perception. Jesus was supremely the man of the Spirit (3.22; 4.1, 14, 18), and, as such, was able to heal and restore broken human lives. The preaching and healing of the apostles can begin only when they have received the same power (Acts 1.8).

What were the gifts of the Spirit according to Luke? In this respect there is a notable consistency in his work. The Spirit is the spirit of prophecy, wisdom and power. He enables people to see more deeply into things; to penetrate more deeply into the will and purpose of God, to see into the heart of man, and, as a result, to be able to predict and speak authoritatively about the direction in which events are moving. That is the gift of prophecy, examples of which are very many in Luke's work.[1]

This gift is closely related to that of wisdom. There is a knowledge of life, man and God which is more than a match for would-be opponents, and yet is not necessarily derived from, or dependent on, cleverness (see, for example, Luke 2.40–52; 21.15; and Acts 4.13f.; 6.10 and 7.10). And, thirdly, the Spirit confers power. That power, of course, is primarily a healing power, but it is also a power which may judge and destroy (Acts 5.1–11; 13.6–12).

Luke's understanding of the Spirit has been influenced by the Old Testament, where the Spirit of God is often represented as a force taking hold of a person and driving him to say and do things normally beyond him. It is a power for which the disciples of Jesus must pray, for without it they cannot re-present, either in word or deed, the message of the cross and resurrection.

So far we find a remarkable consistency running throughout Luke-Acts. A more varied picture emerges when we consider when and how a person receives the Spirit. Normally the Spirit is given at baptism (e.g. Acts 2.38), but that is not always so. In the story of Simon Magus, he and the Samaritans are baptized some time before they receive the Spirit (8.16), whilst in the case of Cornelius and his friends, it is the other way round (10.44–48). In the first instance consistency has probably been sacrificed in the interests of the story; in the second, Luke wanted to emphasize that on this momentous occasion it was God who was 'calling the tune'. There is a similar variety within Acts in the references to the laying on of hands. The Spirit is conferred by this means at 8.17 and 19.6, but not elsewhere.

When we turn to what Paul has to say about the Holy Spirit, we undoubtedly find common ground with Luke. Prophecy, for example, is the gift of the Spirit (I Cor. 12.10). But there are also different emphases and understandings. Unlike Luke, Paul did not distinguish clearly between the resurrection of Christ and 'Pentecost'. In fact, 'the Spirit of Christ' and 'the Holy Spirit' are vitually interchangeable terms, whereas Acts 16.6f. seems to offer the only instance of this in Luke's work. Secondly, whereas Luke portrayed the Spirit as a supernatural force, coming upon a person from outside himself, Paul's language is more 'inward'. Some of the situations for which he was writing obliged him to emphasize the moral implications of life in the Spirit. To the Galatians, wavering between the extremes of rules and ritual on the one hand and licentious freedom on the other, he wrote of the fruit of the Spirit (Gal. 5.22f.). To the Corinthians, living in an atmosphere of heady, unbalanced enthusiasm, he argued, in a highly polemical chapter, that love was far more important than more spectacular gifts (I Cor. 13).

The writer of the Fourth Gospel, like Paul, makes no clear distinction between the resurrection and Pentecost (John 20), but in other respects he is closer to Luke than to Paul. The most striking feature of what this Gospel has to say about the Holy Spirit lies in the parallels drawn between Jesus and the Spirit. ('Paraclete' and 'the Spirit of Truth' are the favourite Johannine terms.) Almost all that John says of the Spirit, he says also of Jesus, who was to the disciples during his lifetime what the Spirit is to them now. Indeed he is, in some ways, more to them than Jesus could be, for he was alongside them, whereas the Spirit will be in them (John 14.17). This does not make the Spirit superior to Jesus, for without the cross and resurrection, leading to the Son's return to the Father, the Spirit could not be given.

Another important parallel lies in the relationships between the Father and the Son, and between the Son and the Spirit. For example, the Son bears witness to the Father (e.g. 3.11), speaking not his own, but the Father's words (12.49f.), and similarly the Spirit bears witness to Christ, bringing to the disciples the words of Christ (15.26; 14.26). Here we are far nearer to the later doctrine of the Trinity than we appear to be in Luke-Acts, although we should not forget the many close parallels, noted in the last chapter, between Jesus and the apostles. The language of Luke and John may be very different, but on this point there is no divergence: 'As the Father sent me, so I send you' (John 20.21). On the whole, however, Luke, Paul and John describe the power and work of the Holy Spirit in quite different ways. Their fundamental agreement lies in a common understanding that it was Jesus alone who had made possible the age of the Spirit in which they lived, and, secondly, the Spirit's presence and power bore the character of Jesus.

When we turn to the subject of the Christian's discipleship in the world, the same variety can be seen both within Luke-Acts and elsewhere in the New Testament. We noted in Chapter 3 that Luke did not believe that the command to the disciples to forgo their possessions (Luke 14.33) applied literally to all Christians. Different patterns of discipleship are portrayed. Ministry and service might be expressed in generosity with what one has, and by hospitality, or by giving up all one's possessions (or a large part of them) to the poor, or, alternatively, by sharing everything completely with one's fellow Christians.[2] Whatever the response, a person's attitude to and disposal of his possessions seems to have been, for Luke, the acid test of commitment and obedience.

The writings of Luke contain more teaching about the use of wealth than any other books in the New Testament. Two other passages in other writers, however, may be noted here. On the one hand, the Letter of James condemns the rich in language reminiscent of Amos and Isaiah (James 5.1–6). If these verses refer to the prevailing social and economic conditions, they comprise one of the very few New Testament passages which condemn social injustice. On the other hand, the First Letter to Timothy, whilst recognizing the dangers and transience of wealth, acknowledges the presence of rich people in the community to which it was addressed. The writer advises them not to renounce everything, but to be generous (I Tim. 6.17–19).

The conclusion to be drawn from the variety of teaching within the New Testament about possessions is simple, yet important: nothing less than total commitment is required of every disciple, but its practical consequences may take many forms.

The third theme to be considered here is apostleship. What was the significance of 'apostles' in the age of the Spirit? We have seen how important in Luke's scheme the apostles were. They are the prime witnesses of all that has happened, and especially of the resurrection (Acts 1.22; 2.32, etc.). They are the people who were with Jesus from the beginning, accompanying him from Galilee to Jerusalem (Acts 13.31), and who thus became a symbol of continuity. In Acts the apostles play the part of 'sheet-anchor'. When many other Christians had to leave Jerusalem because of persecution, the apostles remained (8.1), because, in Luke's scheme, it was inconceivable that they should be anywhere else but at the Christian headquarters.

But did that mean Paul was not an apostle? He, after all, had not accompanied Jesus from Galilee to Jerusalem. In one (Acts 14.4) or perhaps two places,[3] Luke does describe Paul as an apostle. This gives the impression that he had momentarily forgotten that in his scheme only the Twelve are apostles, a unique group to which others cannot be added. And so perhaps we should conclude from these verses that, even though Luke formally excluded Paul from that group, he nevertheless could not help thinking of him as an apostle.

The picture presented by Paul is quite different. First, his apostolic status was sharply challenged. He may well have been criticized as a comparative newcomer to the scene; he had certainly not known Jesus in the flesh (II Cor. 5.16). To him, however, that did not matter. He had been commissioned by God and had seen the risen Christ (Gal. 1.15f.; I Cor. 9.1), and that was sufficient. One consequence of this is that, in Paul's writings, the apostles comprise a group more numerous than 'the Twelve', including, for example, Andronicus and Junias (Rom. 16.7), two people referred to only here in the New Testament.

Secondly, Paul saw the role of an apostle rather differently from Luke. In his view, so far from being a 'sheet-anchor', an apostle was a pioneer and trailblazer, preaching the gospel where it had not yet been heard (Rom. 15.20; I Cor. 1.17). Although the continuing care of the churches he founded was naturally his concern as well, as his letters testify, other people had the task of consolidating his work after him. He himself had to keep moving, because time was short.

It is impossible and unnecessary to reconcile Luke's view of an apostle with that of Paul. Other New Testament writings increase the variety still further. The Gospel of Matthew contains the well-known commission to Peter (16.16–18), but the word 'apostle' appears only once (10.2). The Fourth Gospel, on the other hand, has been thought by some scholars to represent a reaction against the emphasis of others upon the apostolic office. This is by no means certain, particularly in view of John 20.21–23, although an 'apostle' is put firmly in his place in the one verse where that word occurs (13.16).

Some of the later writings of the New Testament deal with the question of what was apostolic and what was not. It is very likely that the Letters to Timothy and to Titus were written, not by Paul himself – although they may contain fragments of his letters – but by a disciple of Paul. The author used Paul's name rather than his own in the sincere belief that he was saying what the apostle might have said in the same circumstances. He tried, therefore, to be faithful to the teaching and spirit of Paul. To this we may add that a person could be considered apostolic only if he himself had been faithful to the teaching and spirit of Jesus. It is here, in fact, that we find the underlying unity amongst New Testament writers about this subject. Clearly there was a variety of views within the early churches about the role and even the credentials of an apostle, and Luke's view was no doubt one among several, although it became increasingly influential as time went on. No one, however, disputed the fact that the supreme reference-point for determining the authority and mission of an apostle was Jesus himself.

Lastly, in this section, we consider briefly the statement of three New Testament writers about the future, and particularly about the return of Christ. Paul believed that the age of the Spirit would be short, for the Spirit was a sign of the last days, a 'first instalment' guaranteeing that Christ would return before long to save and redeem his own completely (e.g. Rom 8.23). There is a trace of this understanding in the Acts of the Apostles (2.17), but on the whole the perspective of Luke is very different. The importance of the interval before the end is much greater because Luke could see that it would be longer than Paul and his contemporaries had anticipated. His advice to his own readers, therefore, was to avoid feverish excitement and speculation about the nearness of the end (Luke 19.11; 21.8), but at the same time to 'be ready', because they do not know when it will be (e.g. Luke 12.40).[4]

John, too, belonged to a generation in which few people still expected the immediate return of Christ. 'The Day of the Lord', which is such a prominent hope in Paul's theology, is not mentioned at all in the Fourth Gospel. The only possible references to Christ's return occur in John 14.3 and 21.23. In this respect John was closer to Luke than to Paul, but he was very different from Luke in the way in which he tended to 'mix' or fuse the past and the present, giving his Gospel an atmosphere of timelessness. This is particularly so in chapters 14 to 17, where the words are attributed to the earthly Jesus, but the situation envisaged is that of the author and his contemporaries.[5] Luke, by contrast, plotted different events at clearly marked intervals along the line of time.

The similarities and differences between these writers in their attitudes to the future exhibit the same pattern which we have observed in other themes. Their theologies cannot be welded together into a systematic whole but, once again, Christ remains the supreme reference-point. Whether history ends tomorrow or goes on for much longer, the future will be determined by him. He has been revealed as both the foundation and the goal of creation.

We have now surveyed what Luke and other writers had to say about the Spirit, the use of possessions, apostleship and the future, particularly the return of Christ. In Luke-Acts we have found considerable variety; none of these subjects was fitted by the writer into a rigid mould, or woven into one consistent pattern. It is equally clear that, in the New Testament as a whole, there is no uniform view on any of these themes. Each writer deals with each of them in his own way in the light of the situation for which he was writing.

But in spite of this diversity it is not difficult to see an overriding unity. There is never any doubt in the New Testament that the Holy Spirit is the Spirit of God and the Spirit of Jesus. Some writers, such as Paul and the author of I John, were at pains to distinguish between true and false manifestations of the Spirit, and they did so by reference to Jesus himself, and particularly to his death. There is also a general agreement that the age of the Spirit in which they lived was inaugurated and made possible only by Jesus.

In the other themes we considered, Jesus was, as it were, the common denominator. The pattern of discipleship may vary; the demand of total commitment to Christ does not. Arguments about apostolic status and authority in the early church were heated and prolonged, and the New Testament reflects some of the tensions and differences which existed. None, however, disputed from whom the apostle's authority was derived or upon whom his life should be modelled. Finally, whatever a writer's expectation of the future might be, the last word undoubtedly lay with Christ.

In short, the New Testament, for all its diversity, points to Jesus as its unifying centre, and it is this which must be the subject of our next section.

(ii) Jesus the centre

Even in what it has to say about Jesus, the diversity of the New Testament must not be overlooked or minimized. Each writer has his own theology and expresses his convictions in his own way. We must begin, as in the last section, with examples of the variety within Luke's own work.

It is likely that in the first century, as in the twentieth, Christians were not unanimous in their views about the human origins of Jesus. Different circles of Christians may have had their own different traditions. Luke seems to have used two such traditions, even though they were not strictly compatible. In this he was following a well-established Old Testament practice, seen, for example, in the presence of two creation stories, not one, in the first two chapters of Genesis. Thus Luke recounted the story of the virgin birth of Jesus, but in ch. 3 thought it worthwhile to include a genealogy tracing back the line of Joseph through David to Adam. The rather awkward addition in v. 23, 'as people thought', may be his own attempt to reconcile the two traditions.

The diversity of Luke-Acts can also be seen in what Luke has to say about Jesus as the Son of God. According to the first two chapters of the Gospel, Jesus was the Son of God from birth. In Luke 3, if the reading of one ancient manuscript is correct, we find a reflection of the belief that Jesus became the Son of God at his baptism: 'My Son art thou; this day I have begotten thee' (v. 23). Thirdly, in one of Paul's sermons in Acts (13.33), Luke uses this same text from the Old Testament (Ps. 2.7) with reference to the resurrection, implying that only then was Jesus 'crowned' the Son of God. (Psalm 2 was originally a coronation psalm.) There is a trace of this last belief about Jesus in Paul (Rom. 1.4), where the apostle was probably quoting part of an earlier creed.

What is the significance of this bewildering variety? It means that Luke-Acts probably reflects something of the theological development of the first century. Not only did the convictions of Christians about Jesus vary, but also their views developed as time went on. In the long run most Christians concluded that it was more satisfactory to speak of Jesus as the Son of God from birth, and, later still, as the Son 'begotten before all worlds'. But this was the result of much thought over quite a long period of time.

It would be wrong, however, to think of Luke's teaching about Jesus as an untidy mass of contradictions. There is a steady emphasis throughout his work that Jesus is the bringer of salvation, the one who puts into effect the decisive, crowning stage of God's plan for the world. There is also never any doubt that the God of Jesus was the God of the Old Testament, or that the risen Christ was anyone other than the Jesus who had lived and been crucified.

We turn now to look at Luke's understanding of Jesus against the background of other New Testament writings. How distinctive were his ideas, and what had he in common with other writers? The discussion must necessarily be limited, and here we shall consider the birth, death, resurrection and ascension of Jesus.

It is well known that only Luke and Matthew in the New Testament refer to a virgin birth. The silence of the other writers on the subject means one of three things: either they did not know of it, or they knew of it but did not think it important or relevant for their writing, or they knew of it but rejected it. Whichever view we take, it is difficult to deny that the New Testament confirms the diversity amongst first-century Christians to which the Gospel of Luke alerted us.

On the other hand, Luke-Acts is silent about the 'pre-existence' of Christ. Paul wrote of Christ as the agent of God in creation: '. . . there is one Lord Jesus Christ, through whom all things came to be, and we through him' (I Cor. 8.6). John, even more explicitly, referred to the glory shared by the Father and the Son before creation (John 17.5), and attributed to Jesus the claim, 'Before Abraham was I am' (8.58). Did Luke, then, not believe this? It is impossible to say, but it is more likely that he chose other ways of expressing his own theology. The nearest equivalent in his writings to this theme, although it is not to be equated with it, is his emphasis on the witness of the Old Testament to Christ (e.g. Luke 24.27, 44). This is a point also made – and more clearly made – by Paul and John.

Thus, on the subject of the origins and pre-existence of Jesus, we find the same diversity which we have found to exist in other areas. Luke wrote about a virgin birth; no other New Testament writer except Matthew referred to it. Others described Christ in 'pre-existent' language which Luke did not use at all. Yet underlying this variety are two basic convictions. First, God was in Christ from the very beginning, and if the virgin birth is rejected as a historical event, it may nevertheless be interpreted as a symbol of this. Secondly, if that line of thought is pursued still further, God did not *become* Christlike at the dawn of the New Testament period; this had been his character in the history of Israel and even 'before all worlds'. That is the importance of the fulfilment of scripture and of pre-existence language.

Luke's understanding and presentation of Jesus' death is both distinctive and varied. There is no cry of dereliction from the cross; here Luke differs from both Mark and Matthew (Mark 15.34; Matt. 27.46). There is also very little sacrificial language: Luke 22.19f., if Luke wrote these verses, and Acts 20.28 are the only exceptions. It seems that he avoided such language since, apparently, he chose to omit Mark 10.45 with its reference to 'a ransom for many'.[6] In this respect he is very different from several other writers, notably Paul and the writer of the Letter to the Hebrews, who frequently depict Christ's death as a sacrifice. Instead, Luke emphasized that the cross was the only route by which the Messiah could enter his glory; it was foreshadowed in scripture and, as his use of *dei* shows, it was part of God's will and purpose (see, for example, Luke 18.31; 24.26).

There is also another feature of Luke's work to be noted here. From time to time in his writings he invited his readers to see a parallel between Jesus and Moses. This may have been intended in his account of the transfiguration in his addition of the Greek word *exodos* (Luke 9.31), meaning not only 'exodus' but also 'death', and a word which would inevitably call to mind the 'exodus' of the Hebrews from Egypt. 'Exodus' language is also used in the speech of Stephen in Acts 7. Luke worded some verses in such a way, it seems, as to suggest that Moses' achievements foreshadowed the work of Jesus: 'He thought his fellow-countrymen would understand that God was offering them deliverance through him, but they did not understand' (v. 25); 'It was Moses who led them out, working miracles and signs in Egypt' (v. 36). Luke, therefore, thought of the cross as the means of a second and greater exodus by which the Messiah would lead his people to life (Acts 3.15).

The absence of references to the cross in some of the sermons in Acts might suggest that for Luke it was not as important as the resurrection, which is invariably mentioned. Even when Luke does refer to the death of Jesus, he often does so quite briefly (e.g. Acts 2.23, 36). Nevertheless, his recognition that even this event fell within, and not outside, the plan and purpose of God implies an understanding of grace reminiscent of the note on which the book of Genesis ends. The story of Joseph was, in essence, the story of an innocent man whose sufferings were the means of preserving many lives: 'You meant to do me harm; but God meant to bring good out of it by preserving the lives of many people, as we see today' (Gen. 50.20).

Luke and Paul undoubtedly shared much common ground in their understanding of the cross. Both recognized that it was the means of new life, although Paul's thinking here is the more profound and detailed of the two writers. Both also believed the cross to be the work of God, the language of Paul, again, being more varied and complex than that of Luke. According to Paul the cross is the means of freedom from the Law, from sin and from death; it is the means of reconciliation to God and of expiating sin; it is the revelation of God's love and, in spite of appearances to the contrary, a triumphal procession.[7] The circumstances for which Paul was writing were partly responsible for the differences between himself and Luke. His conflict over the question about the terms on which Gentiles should be admitted into the new Israel forced him to think through the implications of the cross in a way

that no one else had done before him. The challenges to his apostleship
at Corinth, and the failure of Christians there to grasp the implications
of the cross for Christian life and conduct, once again obliged him to
emphasize 'Christ crucified'. Finally, in the Letter to the Romans,
regarded by many as Paul's theological testament, the apostle made it
clear (3.21ff.; 8.31ff.) that the death of Jesus was the supreme evidence
that God had declared himself for man and freely justified him, irre-
spective of his moral attainments.

The language and ideas of John's Gospel are different again. Jesus is
described as 'the Lamb of God, who takes away the sin of the world'
(1.29), the Good Shepherd who lays down his life for the sheep (10.15),
and the one who must die not only for the Jewish nation, but also in
order that 'the scattered children of God may be gathered into one'
(11.51f.). The most distinctive feature of the Fourth Gospel, however,
is the way in which the cross is understood as Jesus' exaltation, rather
than his humiliation or rejection (which, on the whole, is the viewpoint
of Luke and Paul).[8] The way in which the evangelist uses the words
'lift up' and 'glorify' offers the clearest example of this. John's language
is often ambiguous, intended to be understood on two levels. Thus,
when he wrote, 'This Son of Man must be lifted up' (3.13), and, 'I shall
draw all men to myself, when I am lifted up from the earth' (12.32), he
was referring to both the cross and the resurrection. Similarly, when he
wrote, 'The hour has come for the Son of Man to be glorified' (12.23),
he intended his readers to see that the cross and resurrection together
were the supreme manifestation of God's glory. The cross, for John,
was 'Jesus' finest hour',[9] as the final cry of triumph indicates: 'It is
accomplished!' (19.30).

The Letter to the Hebrews provides yet another distinctive way of
understanding the death of Jesus. Scholars have frequently noted the
words and ideas common to this letter and to Luke-Acts. This is true to
some extent of their understanding of the cross: 'Jesus who, for the sake
of the joy that lay ahead of him, endured the cross, making light of its
disgrace, and has taken his seat at the right hand of God' (Heb. 12.2).
This verse, however, does not indicate the main thrust of the argument
of Hebrews. Jesus, according to this writer, was not only the Son of
God, but also 'High Priest for ever, in the succession of Melchizedek'
(e.g. 5.6). His death, therefore, is understood as the perfect offering of
a sinless high priest, who thus presents himself as a sacrifice 'once for
all' (e.g. 9.12, 14 and 27). As we have seen, there is no more than a vague
allusion to these ideas in Luke's work.

It is clear, then, that the New Testament contains a variety of ways of interpreting the cross. The different interpretations often overlap, and there is often a common use of the same Old Testament texts, but, as with other themes we have studied in this chapter, it is neither necessary nor possible to fit all the differences into a single, systematic whole. It is impossible to speak of 'the New Testament doctrine of the cross', for there is no single doctrine or understanding of it.

Luke's own interpretation of the cross seems less rich and profound than those of the other writers we have considered. It also occupies a less prominent place. But, unlike much of the work of Paul and the Letter to the Hebrews, Luke-Acts was not intended to be primarily a treatise on the cross, and what it says about the death of Jesus should not be taken in isolation from his life, of which it was both the summary and the climax.

Finally, in this section we consider Luke's understanding of the resurrection in relation to those of other New Testament writers. It must be admitted at once that Christians are divided about faith's 'minimum requirement' here. Many take it for granted, and some argue passionately that a Christian must believe, that Christ's resurrection was a physical, objective event. In the final section of Chapter 3 I argued that this is not the only possible view. The conviction that God affirmed or vindicated Jesus beyond death *is* essential to Christian faith; on this all New Testament writers are agreed. But, once again, there is no single interpretation or understanding of the resurrection, still less any 'agreed statement' about the manner or form of it.

Luke and John are the two New Testament writers most responsible for the widely held view that the Bible demands belief in the physical resurrection of Christ. In their Gospels the risen Jesus eats bread and fish, invites Thomas to put his hand into his side, and so on. Three points, however, should be borne in mind. First, I pointed out in Chapter 3 that the narratives which describe resurrection appearances were not straightforward historical accounts of what actually happened. Whilst some experiences or happenings (I Cor. 15.3–8 is the earliest evidence we have) gave rise to the conviction that Jesus lived again, these narratives must not be understood simply as offering 'proof' of the resurrection. It would be equally, if not more, true to say that the experience and reality of the resurrection contributed to the development of the stories.

Secondly, the situations for which Luke and John were writing should not be forgotten. As time went on it became increasingly necessary to emphasize that the risen Christ was none other than the one who had been crucified. (The scandal of death by crucifixion was such that there were many who preferred a Christian faith with a resurrection and no cross.) It is possible that the two evangelists did this by the vivid 'physical' details of their final chapters.

Lastly, as we saw earlier, Paul preferred to write of the resurrection in spiritual terms. The resurrection body, according to him, would not be a physical entity (I Cor. 15.35ff.). It must be frankly acknowledged, however, that our categories of thought were not his, and it may be wrong to attribute to him the modern distinction between 'spiritual' and 'physical'. A further example of the diversity of the New Testament on this subject is provided by the Letter to the Hebrews. There the language of resurrection hardly ever occurs. The author preferred instead to write of Jesus' exaltation to the right hand of God. What mattered supremely for him was that our high priest should be in the heavenly temple 'on our behalf' (9.24).

Before we examine the still greater variety within the New Testament on this subject, we must consider some of the leading ideas in Luke-Acts. First, Luke's approach is the most historical of all the New Testament writers. The appearances of the risen Christ are described as 'proofs' (Acts 1.3), and occurred over a period of forty days. This emphasis upon 'proof' was taken to extremes in later times (and still is) on the mistaken assumption that if only the resurrection could be proved to people, they would automatically believe. But nowhere in Luke's writings does the resurrection remove the need for faith; on the contrary, it is the indispensable basis of faith. The invitation to faith could only be issued because God had raised Jesus from the dead (Acts 2.36–38). Not surprisingly, therefore, Luke emphasized the witness of the apostles to the resurrection, as anyone was bound to do who, like him, was conscious of the growing gap in time between Christian origins and his own day. One further feature of his historical approach, as we have noted before, is his presentation of the resurrection and ascension as two separate events. Elsewhere in the New Testament there is no such distinction, but for him there had to be a definite point in time at which the risen Christ ascended to the right hand of God, and after which Jesus was not seen on earth. Lastly, we may note the way in which some of the early sermons in Acts (e.g. 3.14f.) present the resurrection as God's reversal of man's verdict upon Jesus. It was his supreme vindication of the Messiah.

When we turn to other New Testament writers, interpretations, as usual, vary. A dominant concept in the letters of Paul is that, 'the life I now live is not my life, but the life which Christ lives in me' (Gal. 2.20). Paul alluded to his own vision of the risen Christ, and to the tradition he had received of Christ's appearances to others (I Cor. 15.3–8), but more frequently he wrote of experiencing what he called 'the power of his (i.e. Christ's) resurrection' (e.g. Phil. 3.10). This was the necessary counterpart to his teaching about the cross. Death and resurrection were the definitive pattern of Christian – and therefore apostolic – living. Thus, although the contrast must not be exaggerated, Paul's emphasis is more experiential or existential; unlike Luke, for instance, he did not need to dwell on the importance of the apostolic witness to the resurrection except in I Cor. 15, since there were still alive many who, like himself, had seen the risen Christ.

The Gospel of Mark remains something of an enigma. Almost all scholars are agreed that 16.9–20 is a later addition to the original Gospel. But if that is so, did the Gospel have an account of a resurrection appearance which was lost at an early stage of its transmission? Or did the writer intend to finish abruptly, and even cryptically, 'They said nothing to anybody, for they were afraid' (v. 8)? If he did, this does not mean that Mark regarded the resurrection itself as unimportant. He had already made it clear that God would vindicate Jesus (e.g. 8.31), and so his final section need contain only a brief allusion to the tradition of the empty tomb. But it is probable that the conclusion of the Gospel should be interpreted as a call to faith. 'Galilee' (16.7) here could be a symbol of the Gentile world (compare Matt. 4.15), but whether it is or not, an invitation and a promise to faith lie in the words 'you will see him there'. We may therefore venture the tentative conclusion that Mark, unlike Luke, did not wish to make the account of a resurrection appearance the climax of his work.

It has been suggested that John need not have added ch. 20 to his Gospel, since for him, as we saw, the cross itself was Jesus' exaltation. But by the time he wrote, stories of resurrection appearances must have been so widely known and valued that it would have been unthinkable to leave them out completely. In any case, John wished to make his own points. Jesus' resurrection was his return to the Father. Now, for the first time in this Gospel, God is described not just as the God and Father of Jesus, but as 'my Father and your Father, my God and your God' (20.17). The same verse, with its command to Mary 'Do not cling to me', may be intended as an injunction to every disciple not to cling to, or seek after, tangible proof of the resurrection, since Jesus' return to the Father would enable his presence to continue in a new and deeper way – in the Spirit. Here, too, is an interpretation of the resurrection different from that of Luke.

Thus with the resurrection, as with all the themes we have reviewed in this section, we find a variety of interpretations within the New Testament. Early Christians clearly differed in their emphases, and may even have disagreed about the manner and nature of Christ's resurrection. But they were united in their conviction that God had raised Jesus from the dead, and that the same Jesus was the one who had been crucified. In short, the New Testament invites us to believe in Christ crucified and raised to God's right hand (defined by Luther as 'everywhere'). It does not thrust upon us any single, exclusive understanding of his birth, death or resurrection. In the last section of this chapter we must consider briefly the implications of these findings.


### (iii) Conclusion

'Does the Bible contradict itself?' It is a question which has been asked many times, and Christians have often expended much energy in arguing that it does not. I hope that this chapter has indicated a different approach to the 'contradictions' within the Bible. 'Contradiction' is, in fact, a misleading word. It would be more accurate to talk about a diversity within the New Testament which can serve as a model for our ecumenical age.

'Unity without uniformity' has been one of the most popular slogans in movements towards Christian unity. It should now be clear that this can be said of the New Testament documents themselves. The church eventually determined that these books – no more, no less – should comprise a 'canon', or norm, by which successive Christian generations might find their bearings in matters of faith and conduct. This means that the New Testament itself sanctions Christian diversity, but at the same time sets limits to that diversity.[10] For example, not all first-century Christians, as we have seen, seem to have believed in the virgin birth, or to have thought of the resurrection in exactly the same way. On the other hand, no document in the New Testament suggests that a Christian may believe in the resurrection without taking seriously the implications of the cross. Paul, because of the situation at Corinth, was fully alive to the danger of misinterpreting the resurrection, and both the epistles to Corinth were written, partly at least, to deal with this problem. Similarly, no Christian could or can deny that Jesus was a human being of flesh and blood and still remain within the sphere of diversity approved by the New Testament.

The unifying centre of the New Testament is Jesus himself. He is the supreme authority and reference point. The Fourth Gospel calls him '*the* Word', the one to whom the words of each writer point. This means that a Christianity without Jesus is both absurd and impossible. That may sound obvious, and yet it is easy to call a religious faith 'Christian', even though its real basis is a fairly conventional morality, and its focus of devotion a church rather than Christ himself. But even 'Jesus' may be a convenient name or symbol on to which we project our own opinions and prejudices. Hans Küng, in his book *On Being a Christian*, has illustrated this well enough in a section called 'Which Christ?'.[11] In this matter, too, the New Testament provides guidelines and controls. It is the Jesus witnessed to by these documents who is the author and centre of Christian faith. But here, too, there is diversity. We are offered, not one portrait of Jesus, but four. These, together with the other New Testament documents, constitute the touchstone for understanding and interpreting his life, death and resurrection. To this rich diversity the writings of Luke make a vital contribution.

# CONCLUSION

# Reading Luke-Acts Today

The aim of this book has been to indicate something of the background, contents and purpose of Luke-Acts by drawing on the insights of modern New Testament scholarship. It has been written in the conviction that such insights can greatly enrich and illuminate our reading of the New Testament, if we will allow them to do so. It is easy, however, to underestimate the difficulties of such reading. Some passages are so familiar that the problems contained in them may be overlooked, while others are too readily modernized or made relevant in a way which does violence to their original meaning. It may be useful, therefore, to conclude this survey by a brief consideration of this question. We shall concentrate on the writings of Luke, but clearly much of what can be said about reading Luke-Acts also applies to the rest of the New Testament.

First, it cannot be over-emphasized that Luke was writing for first-century people with their situation and problems in his mind. When this is forgotten, the point of a passage may be obscured or blunted. One of the most important examples of this in the whole of the New Testament is the controversy over circumcision, discussed by Paul in his letter to Galatia and referred to by Luke in Acts 15. The issue was whether trust and commitment alone made a person a Christian, or whether a 'qualification', such as submitting to an external ritual, was necessary first. A more obvious example from elsewhere in the New Testament lies in the command, 'Wives obey your husbands'. In one place where it occurs (I Peter 3.1), it is clear from the context that what is really being said is, 'If you are the only Christian in your family, live in such a way as to bring the rest of the family to faith'. In the first century that involved accepting some, at least, of the conventions of the time.

It is important, therefore, not to modernize Luke, or to wrench his writings out of their historical context. It can be done all too easily, by attributing to him, for example, later doctrines and practices of the church, or by reading our own ideas into his writings. The distinction between reading meanings into a book of the New Testament and reading them out of it is often a fine one, but it is vital. In the first instance we are foisting upon the author our own opinions or, even worse, our prejudices; in the second, we are finding illumination – and new meanings – by discovering, as far as we can, what the author originally meant.

If Luke was writing for first-century people, we should not expect him to be easily comprehensible, still less immediately relevant. The gap between his time and ours, with all their differences of mental outlook, culture and theology, requires from us an effort to understand his work. And because he wrote in and for a particular situation, we should expect that different parts of his writings will speak to different people at different times. It is better to set a passage on one side, rather than read into it a message totally at variance with its contents. Lastly, in this respect, we should not expect Luke to answer our problems, although we may justifiably hope that reading him will help us towards finding our own answers.

One important way to guard against the misuse of Luke-Acts is to put questions to the texts which are studied. What the right questions are will vary according to the contents, but these are some which are relevant for studying any passage:

What is the writer trying to say?

Is it possible to describe, or to imagine, the kind of situation he is addressing?

What experience, and what convictions, lie behind this passage?

What may we learn from the way in which the writer and his church saw things, tackled their problems, thought things out?

A further question inevitably arises in a survey of this kind. What authority can or should Luke-Acts possess for modern readers? The question can be misleading because there are different kinds of authority. That of the New Testament stems from the Christ to whom the documents bear witness. Its authority, therefore, is like Christ's, but derived from and subordinate to him. The relevance of this for reading the New Testament is this: when the Gospels say that Jesus taught with authority, they do not mean that he had a licence to teach, but that his authority was of a more personal kind which could not be proved or disproved, but only encountered and experienced. The same is true of the writings of Luke, the authority of which must be a personal discovery, rather than the subject of discussion. That discovery can only be made by reading and listening to the documents themselves with the openness and humility which are akin to prayer.

# BIBLIOGRAPHY

The following commentaries are recommended for further study of St Luke's Gospel and the Acts of the Apostles:

G. B. Caird, *The Gospel of St Luke*, Penguin Books 1963
J. Drury, *Luke*, Fontana Books 1973
E. E. Ellis, *The Gospel of Luke*, Oliphants 1966
I. H. Marshall, *The Gospel of Luke*, Paternoster 1978
E. Haenchen, *The Acts of the Apostles*, Blackwell 1971
R. P. C. Hanson, *The Acts of the Apostles*, Oxford University Press 1967
C. S. C. Williams, *The Acts of the Apostles*, A. & C. Black 1957

Of these, the Marshall and Haenchen commentaries are much more detailed than the rest.

The following studies of Luke-Acts are recommended for further reading:

C. K. Barrett, *Luke the Historian in Recent Study*, Epworth Press 1961
H. Conzelmann, *The Theology of Saint Luke*, Faber & Faber 1960
J. Drury, *Tradition and Design in Luke's Gospel*, Darton, Longman & Todd 1976
E. Franklin, *Christ the Lord*, SPCK 1975

# NOTES

## 1 Introduction: The Writings of Luke in Recent Scholarship

1. E.g. S. G. Wilson, *Luke and the Pastoral Epistles*, SPCK 1979.

2. Compare the words of John the Baptist in Matt. 3.7–10 with those in Luke 3.7–9; in the Greek there is a difference of only one word.

3. This is true if Gal. 2 refers to the same meeting as Acts 15. This is likely, but it means that Luke has one visit too many (Acts 9.26; 11.30).

4. This is not the view of all scholars, but the evidence is set out in an essay by Vernon K. Robbins in *Perspectives on Luke–Acts*, edited by C. H. Talbert, T. & T. Clark 1978, pp. 115–42.

5. The rising of Theudas and his followers took place between AD 44 and AD 46, and that of Judas before that, probably in AD 6. There is an additional difficulty about the census, mentioned here and also in Luke 2.1: see Chapter 2 on this.

6. See the brief bibliography for details of publishers, etc., of this and other books mentioned in this chapter.

7. Goulder believes that the Greek word *kathexēs*, translated in the AV as 'in order' and in the NEB as 'connected narrative', carries the implication that Luke's Gospel was to be read as part of a lectionary cycle in church.

8. Luke's largest omission, as we noted earlier, is Mark 6.45–8.26, much of which Luke may well have thought unsuitable for his readers, if they were predominantly Gentile (e.g. Mark 7.1–30).

9. Luke has a much shorter sermon which begins and ends in the same way as the Sermon on the Mount (Luke 6.20–49), but of the rest of Matthew's sermon some sections are to be found in several different places in Luke, whilst others are missing altogether.

10. See, for example, the preface to G. B. Caird's otherwise straight-forward commentary.

## 2 From Nazareth to Jerusalem

1. This is not to say that he was a Jew. He may well have been a 'proselyte', a Gentile who had adopted the Jewish faith.

2. Some scholars, notably C. H. Dodd, have argued that the wording of Luke in these verses derives largely from Old Testament prophecies, and so they were not necessarily written with the disaster of AD 70 in mind. It is possible that they come from a Christian tradition well before AD 70, but Luke almost certainly wrote after that date, and must have written the words with the latest destruction of Jerusalem in his mind's eye.

3. *Saint Luke*, Pelican Gospel Commentaries, p. 34.

4. Although the Romans carried out similar censuses elsewhere, there is no record of a census like this in Judaea. There is also a problem about the reference to Quirinius (2.2), since, according to both Luke and Matthew, Jesus was born in the reign of Herod the Great, who died before Quirinius' governorship. There is no clear solution to this problem: it seems likely that Luke simply made a mistake here.

5. The word 'poor' had many connotations for a Jew. It could mean someone who was destitute, but in the Old Testament it was often used to describe the pious man who in his need cast himself on God.

6. The oldest manuscripts of Luke's Gospel are divided: some have 'seventy' and some 'seventy-two'. Both numbers would have had a symbolic meaning, since, according to Gen. 10, there were seventy Gentile nations, and according to another tradition, there were seventy-two languages in the world. If Luke wrote 'seventy', however, the clue to the meaning of the number may lie in Ex. 24 and Num. 11 with their references to the seventy elders of Israel, appointed, according to Numbers, by Moses.

7. These are the boundaries of his middle section, because before and after these points Luke seems to stay fairly close to Mark. In between them, his material comes mostly from other sources.

## 3  The Way of the Messiah

1. This is less clear in translation, but at 19.29, for example, Luke has changed what was a plural verb in Mark into a singular one.

2. The baptism clearly had to come at the beginning, and the crucifixion at the end, but within those boundaries the evangelists seem to have felt free to vary the course of events.

3. A point made by I. H. Marshall in his commentary, p. 411.

4. C. H. Dodd, *The Parables of the Kingdom*, p. 30.

5. J. D. M. Derrett, *Law in the New Testament*, Darton, Longman and Todd 1970, pp. 48–78.

6. William Temple, quoting or paraphrasing Coleridge, wrote: '. . . the supreme merit of the Gospel is not that it promises forgiveness to those who repent, but that it promises repentance to those who sin' (*Christian Faith and Life*, SCM Press 1931, p. 79).

7. 'Your sins are forgiven you' (e.g. Luke 5.20) was the Jewish way of saying 'God forgives you', not 'I forgive you'. But to say that was to make the shocking claim of speaking for God.

8. For example, Jesus is invited to have a meal with a Pharisee three

times (7.36; 11.37; 14.1), and some Pharisees, according to Acts, became Christians (15.5).

9. The same note of judgment is implied in the story of the Cleansing of the Temple which immediately follows (19.45f.), although there are similar problems about whether it could have happened exactly as the Gospels describe it.

10. Derrett, op. cit., pp. 186–313.

11. *Was Jesus Divine?*, Epworth Press 1979, ch. 2, ii.

12. The term 'apocalyptic' is used to describe a type of Jewish writing which was quite common in the time of Jesus, and which portrayed the future in highly symbolic language, containing a secret message of hope for God's persecuted people. The books of Daniel and Revelation are examples.

13. Not all manuscripts have this verse, as a footnote in the NEB indicates.

14. There is, however, a reference to Christ appearing to 'Simon' (24.34).

## 4  *Luke and the Early Church*

1. Not all manuscripts have the phrase 'and was carried up into heaven' at 24.51.

2. This is part of the meaning behind the symbol of the ascension and the doctrine of the second coming.

3. J. D. G. Dunn, *Jesus and the Spirit*, SCM Press 1975, p. 151.

4. 'Suddenly the Lord whom you seek will come to his temple' (Mal. 3.1).

5. This suggestion was put forward by Philippe Menoud, a French scholar.

6. W. Neil, *The Acts of the Apostles*. However, Acts 2.5 tells against Neil's view (section i above).

7. This decree, which exhorted Gentile Christians 'to abstain from meat that has been offered to idols, from blood, from anything that has been strangled, and from fornication' (v. 29), is not referred to by Paul directly, if at all. It is possible that it comes from a later period, and that Luke read it back into the apostolic age (see also Chapter 5, i).

## 5  *Paul*

1. *The Eternal Now*, SCM Press 1963, p. 142.

2. Some features of this scene imply that Paul was arrested, others do not. Mars' Hill was the place where trials took place before the Council of the Areopagus, but it was also a 'Speakers' Corner'. The truth, as Haenchen suggests in his commentary, is probably that Luke did not wish to define a clear-cut situation, but to create an impression.

3. The meeting with James and the elders (21.18ff.) does not really count in this respect, because of the pressures of the situation in Jerusalem (described in the next section).

4. Compare, for example, v. 34 with I Cor. 4.12; vv. 31, 35 with I Thess. 2.9, 11.

5. This interpretation is more likely than that of NEB, which translated the crucial phrases in vv. 9f. by 'and was picked up for dead', and 'there is still life in him'. The corresponding Greek is more accurately translated 'and was taken up dead', and 'there is life in him', the last phrase being Paul's testimony that he had restored Eutychus to life.

6. The details in vv. 23, 24, 26 are confused, and may reflect a confusion between a purification ritual for people who, like Paul, had travelled abroad and so were thought to be unclean, and the vow known as the vow of the Nazirite, described in Num. 6.1–21 (Haenchen, *Commentary*, pp. 606–14).

7. The dialogue between Paul and the tribune, for instance (21.37–39), seems most improbable in the circumstances.

8. This is the likeliest interpretation of gestures which, in the Old Testament, could be a sign of mourning (e.g. I Sam. 4.12), or rites for averting a curse (e.g. Job 2.12).

## 6  *The Nature and Purpose of Luke's Writings*

1. See Chapter 4, n. 1.

2. Luke probably added what he wanted to say about Paul to an already existing story about a shipwreck. The point of the story is that Paul arrived in Rome only by the providence of God, and Luke, in the manner of ancient writers, spared no literary effort in heightening the drama and importance of what he wished to relate.

3. This challenge may lie behind the defence of the scriptures in II Tim. 3.15–17.

4. I assume here that a disciple of Paul wrote the Letter to the Ephesians.

5. It is strange, however, that Acts 9.36–43 has rather more affinities with Mark's account of the raising of Jairus' daughter than it has with Luke's.

6. Quoted by G. B. Caird, *Saint Luke*, Pelican Books 1963, p. 202.

7. *Luke: Historian and Theologian*, Paternoster Press 1970, e.g. p. 67.

8. *Acts and the History of Earliest Christianity*, SCM Press 1979.

9. I Cor. 7.10; 9.14; 11.23ff. are the only clear allusions to 'commands of the Lord'.

## 7  *Unity without Uniformity: Luke and Other New Testament Writers*

1. See, for example, Luke 1.67; 2.25f.; Acts 11.27f.; 13.1f., 9ff.; 21.9–11.

2. Luke 8.1–3; 10.38; 14.33; 19.8; Acts 2.44f.; 4.32–37.

3. Some, but not all, manuscripts have the word 'apostles' in Acts 14.14.

4. Some scholars think that Paul did not write II Thessalonians, but if he did, his advice in that letter (2.1ff.) is very like that of Luke on this subject.

5. See especially 16.1–4.

6. However, as Morna Hooker points out, Luke might well have replaced Mark 10.32–45 by verses from another source, in what he felt to be a more appropriate setting (Luke 22.24–27).

7. See, for example, Gal. 3.13; Rom. 6.1ff.; II Cor. 5.19; Rom. 3.25; 5.8; Col. 2.14f.

8. I Cor. 1.23–25; Luke 23.42–47, however, are not unlike the thought of John.

9. The phrase is that of Dr David Hill, of Sheffield University.

10. I am indebted here to the excellent discussion of this subject in J. D. G. Dunn, *Unity and Diversity in the New Testament*, SCM Press 1977, esp. pp. 369ff.

11. *On Being a Christian*, Collins 1976, pp. 126ff.

# INDEX

# INDEX